The Big Little Book on Creating

PERSONAL
and FINANCIAL
FREEDOM

DR. ALBERT "ACE" GOERIG

The Big Little Book on Creating Personal and Financial Freedom

For information about this title or to order other books and/or electronic media, contact the publisher:
ACG Press
222 Lilly Rd. NE, Olympia, WA 98506
DoctorAce.com

ISBNs:
979-8-9880408-7-3 (print)
979-8-9880408-8-0 (eBook)

Printed in the United States of America
Cover and Interior design: 1106 Design

TABLE OF CONTENTS

*Go to www.doctorace.com/ to quickly access links to all
the online resources that are referenced in this book.*

About the Author

D Dr. Albert "Ace" Goerig graduated from Case Western Reserve University Dental School and is a retired army colonel. For the past 27 years, he has been both a business and a financial coach to many doctors. In 2004, he wrote his first book: *Time and Money: Your Guide to Personal and Financial Freedom.* His newest book, entitled *The How-to Book on Dividend Growth Investing—Create Generational Wealth and Passive Income for Life!* was published in March 2023. He has a free website, www.doctorace.com with audios and videos to help individuals quickly become debt-free and understand simple and safe investing.

Disclaimer

Foreword and Introduction

*"Dr. Goerig created a masterpiece of financial information
that everyone should have. Rule #1 for this book is READ IT!
You (and your family) will be so glad you did."*

—PHIL TOWN, HEDGE-FUND MANAGER, *NYT* BEST-SELLING AUTHOR
OF *RULE #1, PAYBACK TIME* AND CO-AUTHOR OF *INVESTED.*

As Americans, we live in one of the greatest countries in the world—we can have an incredible life and retire without worrying about money. Most Americans are stressed over their finances and will probably have to keep on working well beyond the retirement age. This is because the Coalition of Four (advertising industry, media, merchants, and banks) and our financial system was designed to take away our freedom and keep us broke and in debt until we die. In this book, I will show you the secrets of getting out of debt quickly and how to invest safely to help you create generational wealth and personal freedom that works.

Everyone I talk to says they want to have wealth and personal freedom. What I find is that more and more people are in worse financial shape today than ever before. The total U.S. consumer debt balance increased to $17.1 trillion in 2023, up 4.4% from $16.38 trillion in 2022. Total revolving debt is $1.32 trillion and has increased 17% over the last four years. In fact, 96% of Americans are prisoners of debt and are slaves to their monthly payments.

The real problem is that most Americans think that always being in debt is normal. The credit card companies—along with the mortgage companies—have trained you in this belief. They have developed a proven profit system that keeps you in debt for a lifetime, so they can steal half of your life's income. You become their cash cow.

In this book, you will learn how to make more than 100% guaranteed return on your money while watching all your debts disappear (even your mortgage) in 5–10 years. How would you like to own everything in your life—your home, your cars, your furniture—everything? How would you like to have no monthly debt payments of any kind, including mortgages, rent, car loans, and credit card payments? Once you are debt free, you will have 50% to 70% of your income available, allowing you to work less, have more time with your family and to live the life of your dreams. And the best part is that you can do it using the money you are currently earning.

This system works for any income level! More importantly, you will learn how to simplify your life and enjoy work more while creating an incredible relationship with your family. The rewards are many. But most of all, I urge you to enjoy the process.

Dr. Albert C. (Ace) Goerig
Olympia, Washington
April 2024

CHAPTER 1

Create an Incredible Life Story

n a May 2017 interview with Charlie Rose, Warren Buffett was asked what gave him his greatest joy. *"That I love going to the office,"* said Buffett. *"It has been my painting for more than fifty years. I get to paint what I want; I own the brush, I own the canvas, and the canvas is unlimited. And that is a pretty nice game, and I get to do it every day with people I like. I don't have to associate with anyone who causes my stomach to turn. If I were in politics, I'd have to smile at a lot of people I'd rather hit. I've got a really good deal, and I am hanging onto it."*

Most of us forget that we have the brush and the canvas, and that we can create our story any way we want. This book will help you through the process of creating your story. We are here on this planet for a relatively brief period, and all we have is from now until the end of our lives. So, how can we make the most of this time?

To live our lives to the fullest, we need to create a new vision or story of what is possible. We all can live the rest of our lives as an exciting adventure. For most of us, because of our cultural context and the lack of training we have received regarding financial matters, it is difficult to set up a guide for reaching financial freedom or even to recognize that our way of relating to money could be very different. However, if we write a story about how we want to live, it is easy to develop and follow a guide to fulfill that story. However, most of us don't know how to develop a coherent and compelling story about financial and personal freedom.

Most Americans want to have more time off to enjoy their family, hobbies, and personal time. They are burdened by long-term debt. Many of them are stressed at work and exhausted when they come home. They are unable to see the possibilities that life has to offer. With the right game plan, they could be debt free within five to ten years and work fewer days a year in a drama-free, stress-free office where they work with the people they like. You may not realize it, but you have the canvas, and you have the brush to create the life of your dreams.

This book was created to help you find the key, to show you the possibilities in your business and personal life and to give you the tools and ideas to create your story. As you go through the book, write down the things you want to change and the steps that you will take to create your new life story. The possibilities are endless.

The best stories are specific *and* flexible—specific in offering a full vision with rich detail, and flexible because life is a process, and we are always growing. As new experiences arise, we begin to see things at a deeper level. When situations change, we need to give ourselves permission to change our minds to stay within our own integrity. You can create a beautiful story that incorporates abundance into your life. Having your finances in order will help support your positive story so you can live life fully. However, writing a life story takes great courage because it involves change. Sometimes you need to change many things to live a free and independent life. In this case, you are called upon to face your fears of confrontation and conflict and to create the life you want. Your story shows the world your intent to change and starts you on your new path. Gandhi was once asked, "What is your message to the world?" He replied, "My life is my message." What is your message to your children?

How to Bring Abundance into Your Life

The reason we create positive stories is to let the universe know what we want. I personally believe that we can bring anything—positive or negative—into our lives, depending on our thoughts. This happens by creating a clear, positive vision of exactly what we want and knowing (believing) that it will come about. More than 100 years ago, in his book *The Science of Getting Rich*,

Wallace Wattles talked about focusing on what you want and not on what you don't want in your life.

We need to put our energies into the creative and not the competitive aspects of life. Never spend any time worrying about what others are doing. Why? Because there is unlimited abundance. If we have the right focus and vision, we can bring whatever we want into our lives. The real fun is helping others create abundance in their lives. I spend little time listening to the negative events in the news, which I cannot control. My real joy and happiness come from relationships with family and in my dental practice. Abundance always comes when we are thankful for all the gifts and richness that we have in our lives.

A Tale of Two Families (Age 25)

Family "A" Earns $72,000 a year.
They have fallen for the scam, and they live big. They buy a big home, expensive cars, and other toys to build their ego and try to make themselves happy while continually creating debt and making monthly payments.

By age sixty, they have paid off their mortgage and school loan, but they still have a second mortgage, car payments, credit cards, and other debts; they have only $80,000 in their retirement account.

Both parents are working full time and resent going into work because they are working just to make their monthly payments. This is reflected in their relationship with their family and co-workers. They will give 2/3 of their life's earnings to their creditors, including interest the taxes paid on that income. Along with that, they will have given up their freedom and a life of choice, which will keep them working for many more years because they *have* to—not because they *want* to.

Family "B" earns $72,000 a year.
They live simply—on one salary—and use the other salary to pay off debt early. They live conservatively, paid cash for used cars, and kept them, which eliminated their car payments. Cars are a terrible investment and are capital intensive. People should buy used cars of good quality and keep them for many years. Not until you are debt free and can afford to buy a car outright with cash should you buy a new car.

In eight years, they are debt free, including all credit cards, cars, mortgages and school loans. At age 33, they have no debt and still live on 1/3 of their income. They now have 60% to 70% of their income to invest for retirement, children's education, vacations, or charitable contributions. They have less stress, and one spouse may choose to work part time only—or be a full-time, stay-at-home parent. They work because they *want* to—not because they *have* to. They have more time for family and friends. They now pay cash for all purchases.

Because they have maximized their retirement Roth 401k and Personal Roth IRA and other personal investments, at age 60, they have more than $10 million in their retirement and are receiving more than $350,000 each year in tax-free passive income from their dividends.

Using the information in this book, you will learn how to be completely debt free in five to ten years. This includes owning their home, cars, and everything else. During that same time, you will learn how to invest in the stock market simply and safely. Initially, you should use paper money while paying off debt and then real money once you understand safe investing. You will share this information with your children so that they can have incredible lives also. Let's begin the adventure.

You Can Become a Millionaire

Here are the lessons from the book *The Millionaire Next Door*, by Thomas Stanley and William Danko. Wealth is not the same as your income. Wealth is what you accumulate (net worth) and not what you spend. Wealth comes from hard work, dedication, planning, and self-discipline. Millionaires do not live in upscale neighborhoods or drive fancy cars. A millionaire's goal is to become financially independent, which is much more important than displaying high social status.

These financially successful people control their consumption and do not allocate too much money to products and services. Millionaires are frugal; they live not only *below* their means—they live *well* below their means. Most millionaires live in an average home and drive a used car; their children go to public schools. They are married to the same spouse, who is also a conservative spender. Warren Buffett, one of the richest men in the world, has lived in the same modest house for more than sixty years, sent his children to public schools, and drives an eight-year-old car.

We all have choices about where we want to spend our money. We could buy a smaller house, go on fewer vacations, buy a smaller car, and put more money into investments. Most people do not consciously sit down and consider their choices; instead, they haphazardly spend their money without focus. Until we are debt free, we are restrained by our income, so we need to create a game plan and focus our excess money to draw up a guide for personal and financial success.

I used to go fishing each year with my brother on the Kenai Peninsula in Alaska. For $200 a day, we would hire an older fishing guide, named Bob. He had a small (14-foot) Lund boat that we would drag out into the ocean and fish for salmon about 100 yards offshore. When he was not guiding, he would drive a school bus during the rest of the year. His wife worked at the post office, and they lived in a small log cabin he built near the ocean.

They lived very conservatively and ate well on salmon and meat from hunting season. Bob died in 2008 at the age of 87. My brother, who was Bob's attorney, was shocked to find that his investment in a Schwab stock market account was more than $8 million. He had most of his money invested in no-load index funds and wonderful dividend growth companies.

If his heirs left that investment portfolio alone, by 2024, it would have grown to more than $40 million, and they would be receiving $1.5 million a year in passive income from dividends. The results of compound interest combined with time become incredible. The ideas in this book can make anyone who is committed to financial freedom a multi-millionaire.

CHAPTER 2

Becoming Debt Free

When all investments are put into perspective, the best returns are from paying off debt and increasing your business profitability. These choices can give you a return of more than 100%. Below are the past 20 years' average returns on various investments.

- **Home: 0–5%.** According to Zillow, while home prices have appreciated nationally at an average annual rate between 3% and 5%, depending on the index used for the calculation, home-value appreciation in different metro areas can appreciate at markedly different rates than the national average. Over time, home values grew about 0% after inflation. Plan on spending 5% of the value of the home to buy it, 10% to sell it, and 1% to 2% a year to maintain it.

- **Average actively managed fund investment:** Investors earned an average of 4.67% on mutual funds over the last 20 years. This is 3.52% less than the average S&P 500 index return.

- **Inflation:** The average inflation rate reported by the U.S. Department of Labor for the United States is 2.8%. In 2022, we saw that rate increase up to 9%. This significantly reduced the return on a 2% bond—by 6%.

- **Short Term Bonds:** Over the past five years, bonds have returned only 1.4% annually. United States Short Term Government Bond Yield was reported at 5.03% in April 2024.

- **S&P 500:** The historical average yearly return of the S&P 500 is 10.3% over the last 100 years, as of end of January 2023. This assumes dividends are reinvested. Dividends account for about 40% of the total gain over this period. Adjusted for inflation, the 100-year average return (including dividends) is 7.214%

- Investing on your own through **Rule One investing** can give you an average return of 15%.

- **Paying off debt:** Up to 300% (3×) return. The secret to financial freedom.

- **Investing in yourself or your business:** Up to 100% increase on return of investment.

You will see how the power of paying off debt can give you a guaranteed return of more than 100% without risk or tax consequence. Everyone needs to focus on what produces the greatest returns. If you execute this game plan right, then you will have more money than you will ever need, which you can trade in for time, freedom, and choices.

Investing in the stock market is not a way to make you rich quickly. It is a way to allow your money to compound over time to provide a very comfortable retirement and become a millionaire. I will introduce you to a program that will teach you the best strategies to safely get the highest returns investing by yourself, without paying the extraordinarily high fees and commissions of financial advisors, brokers, and mutual-fund companies.

Remember that paying off debt first while you increase your income provides the highest returns, with much more predictability than anything you could do by investing in the market.

Why We Pay Off Debt First

1. Easiest and simplest to do and understand.

2. No need for financial advisors and their expensive fees.

3. It can give you a guaranteed 100% return on your money, without risk or taxes.

4. Can be done automatically, right out of your bank account.

5. Changes you from a spender into a saver.

6. Gives you complete peace of mind and choices in your life because no one (banks) owns you.

7. Once debt free, what does it take to live on? Now you have three times the amount of disposable income (previously, 2/3 of your disposable income was paid toward debt and interest payments) to spend on investments and enjoying life.

One of the biggest misconceptions perpetuated by banks and accountants is that you should not pay off your house early, because when you have a mortgage, you can write off the interest rate on your taxes. This allows the banks to continue to get a large amount of interest from using your money.

If you are in the 28% federal income tax bracket and itemize your deductions, you pay one dollar of mortgage interest and save $.28 in taxes. This means you lose $.72 of one dollar to save $.28 in taxes.

Let's look at this closely: In 2024, an average American couple who pays $10,200 a year in interest on their home loan has the choice of either taking the standard deduction of $29,200 or itemizing their return and taking the $10,200 tax write-off. When they itemize, they are unable to take the standard deduction of $29,200 and have an overall loss of $19,000 in standard deduction. The biggest loss is in the interest you paid the bank, which could be more than 200%.

Let us consider a $310,000 mortgage at 4.5% for thirty years. **Mortgage** comes from a French word which **means "death contract."** Below, you can see that, of the first year's loan payment of $18,849, only $5,001 goes to principal, but $13,848 goes to interest, which is lost forever to you. See Figure 1 below. ***This is a 277% loan, not a 4.5% loan.***

In the 28% tax bracket, you had to earn around $17,724 and pay taxes on that to get the $13,847 to give to the bank as interest payments, which makes it a 354% loan. If you pay an additional principal payment of $5,231, you would eliminate one year's payment and save $13,618 in interest; you will have made a 354% return on your money, guaranteed, without risk or any tax consequence (see below).

Year	Interest	Principal	Balance
2024	$13,848	$5,001	$304,999
2025	$13,618	$5,231	$299,768
2026	$13,378	$5,471	$294,297
2027	$13,126	$5,722	$288,575
2028	$12,863	$5,985	$282,590
Total (after 5 years)	**$68,833**	**$27,410**	**$282,590**

The reality: Over the next five years, you would have paid $96,243 in loan payments, and only $27,410 would have gone to pay off the loan. You must understand that the interest is always the highest at the beginning of the loan, and for the first ten years of a 30-year loan, the interest paid will always be more than 100%. Always take advantage of this guaranteed high return.

The bottom line: by paying an additional $5001 toward your mortgage, you eliminate the next year's interest payment of $13,848, which is a guaranteed 277% return on your investment, without risk or tax consequence. With this great return, why would anyone not use the money in their savings (earning less than 1%) to pay off their home? If you are not getting more than a 100% return on your non-tax-deferred stocks, then cash them out, and pay off debts.

When we have debt, saving money is an encoded trap that keeps us poor. In the above example, if you have $100,000 in your savings or non-tax-deferred investments, the best, safest, and highest return on that money is to pay off debt. Paying $100,000 toward the $310,000 home mortgage would drop your mortgage to $210,000 and save you $121,360 in interest payments—while paying off 13 years of the mortgage.

Compare this $121,360 made by paying off debt to the $1,500 you would get with an after-tax return of 1.5% in a 2% bank CD on that same $100,000. You must see the $100,000 put into the house as a high-return, safe, long-term, inflation-adjusted bond. This paid-off asset is always available to you through lines of credit or second mortgages. Once the home is paid off, the money used for mortgage payments becomes a constant source of available cash flow. It is like getting money from a bond.

Today, with the high interest rates, you could pay up to 8% on a mortgage or a school loan. If you paid one more additional payment of $2,506 on a 30-year mortgage 8% loan, you would eliminate $23,909 interest payment and save, or, in other words, make 954% guaranteed without risk and tax free. Because this is after tax dollars, the true percentage is 1363% before taxes. (see chart below)

30 year - $300,000 loan - Real interest rates before and after taxes (24% federal, 6% state tax)										
	At the 30 year		At the 20 Year		At the 15 year		At the 10 year		At the 5 year	
		Real rate		Real rate		Real rate		Real rate		Real rate
Interest rate	Real rate	before taxes	Real rate	before taxes	Real rate	before taxes	Real rate	before taxes	Real rate	before taxes
3.50%	181%	258%	105%	150%	72%	103%	45%	64%	21%	31%
4%	225%	322%	127%	182%	86%	123%	52%	75%	25%	35%
5%	337%	481%	179%	255%	117%	167%	69%	99%	32%	45%
6%	486%	694%	242%	346%	153%	219%	88%	126%	39%	56%
7%	686%	980%	319%	456%	196%	280%	109%	155%	47%	67%
8%	954%	1363%	414%	592%	245%	350%	132%	188%	56%	79%

	30 years		20 Years		15 years		10 year		5 year	
Interest rate	interest	principal	interest	principal	interest	principal	interest	principal	interest	principal
3.50%	10,408	5757	8280	7885	6774	9391	4981	11,184	2846	13,320
4%	11,904	5283	9619	7568	7947	9240	5,904	11,282	3411	13,776
5%	14,899	4426	12,391	6935	10,425	8900	7,904	11,422	4,667	14,659
6%	17,900	3684	15,270	6313	13,068	8516	10,097	11,486	6,090	15,494
7%	20,903	3047	18,239	5711	15,854	8097	12,473	11,478	7,679	16,272
8%	23,909	2506	21,279	5136	18,763	7652	15,015	11,401	9,430	16,985

Debt Is the Devil

It's all about net worth. Our net worth is the total of all our assets, including our investments, bank accounts, and real estate, minus our debts. Paying off debt increases your net worth (wealth) and provides an asset that you can use in emergencies as loan collateral. Paying off debt is a conservative investment strategy. Don't be happy about having more tax deductions, especially when you can't write them off due to the high standard deduction. This is how the government and the banks keep you in debt and in servitude.

Mostly all debt is bad. Debt keeps you imprisoned and prevents you from living a life of freedom, independence, and choice. Being overburdened with financial responsibilities increases your stress; it can damage important and satisfying personal relationships and even lead to divorce, which could cost half of what you own. By changing your spending and saving habits one step at a time, you can regain control of your life. You now know what interest payments really cost you and what to do to change your spending habits.

Some debt can be considered "good" if it has the potential to increase your net worth or significantly enhance your life. A student loan may be considered good debt if it helps you on your career track. Bad debt is money borrowed to purchase rapidly depreciating assets or assets for consumption.

In John Cummuta's excellent audiobook and manual *Transforming Debt into Wealth,* he states, "Every time you make a purchase on credit, you need to consider not just the price you're paying for the product but the price plus interest—plus how much that money could have earned you as an investment."

Based on data from the Federal Reserve Bank of New York and the U.S. Census Bureau (based on 2022 and 2021 data respectively), it can be calculated that each American household carries an average of $7,951 in credit-card debt in a year. The Federal Reserve Bank of New York estimated total credit-card debt for all Americans was $1.13 trillion.

With each debt, the interest you pay puts you on the wrong side of the compound-interest equation. It's important to realize that you are going to make a finite amount of money in your life. If you give too much of it away in interest payments and impulse buying, there will not be enough money left over for you to retire comfortably. You can take two basic approaches with your money: you can spend it on things that don't add meaning to your life, stay in debt, and eat cat food in your retirement years, or you can build your financial future now by paying off debt early and retire early in style.

Every dollar you consume now brings you one dollar of value, but every dollar you use to pay off debt can bring you 5 to 20 times that amount in your retirement years, allowing you to retire 10 to 20 years earlier. Reducing spending and paying off debt will eliminate money problems, improve relationships, and improve your health by reducing stress. And it will serve as a shining example for your children about what is possible.

How would it feel to be out of debt and own your home free and clear, with utilities, taxes, and food as your only real expenses? This is possible for everyone if they're following a clear guide. Most people can pay off all their credit-card debt in one year and their car in the second year. By the third year, they're making extra payments toward their mortgage. Most people can be totally debt free within five to ten years and thereby eliminate payments on student loans, home loans, and business debts.

When you become debt free, there is no need to worry about your credit score or credit report, because you pay cash for all your purchases. *The ability to obtain credit is what got you into trouble in the first place.* The idea that you need to build up your credit by borrowing is an illusion that keeps you in debt. Once you become debt free, no one owns you, and this is true freedom.

Steps to Eliminate Debt

Eliminating debt is a crucial first step in my game plan. The only debt that is reasonable to incur is for the purchase of very large items, such as your house, your education, or your car. Never go into debt for anything else, especially not for consumable items.

I can't state it any more clearly: consumption debt is bad, bad, bad, and bad. The best strategy is to spend less than you make and to save a substantial amount of your money. Then you can consume with saved dollars.

Most families in America are imprinted to use their credit cards and consume, whether they have the money to pay for something or not. If you do this, you typically pay high interest rates; this is not an effective way to manage your money. It is not a bad idea to start cutting up all credit cards except one that you may need. Use a debit card instead of a credit card. For a step-by-step approach to eliminating debt quickly, we can use the debt-elimination worksheet in **Appendix A** at the end of the book.

Once you've made a commitment toward financial freedom and debt reduction, it's important to act by freeing up money from unnecessary expenditures. Change your spending habits, and use only cash, checks, or debit card to buy things. Use the 48-hour rule: For any purchase greater than $100, wait 48 hours to see if you really want to purchase that product. Most times, you will not.

Give yourself a set amount to spend each month so you get the feeling of what this is like. As an experiment, don't do *any* shopping for one month except for food. You may go through an initial withdrawal period. Facing your fears will help you to become wealthy. The way to stop salespeople from trying to sell you something is to simply say, "I can't afford that." If they persist, simply repeat your answer.

While you're reducing expenditures, be sure not to make any major purchases, such as a new car or boat, remodeling, or a new house. Until you are debt free, buy only used cars, and pay cash. Once you are debt free, you can buy a new car but only pay cash. Don't buy a boat until you are debt free. I have had many great boats in my life, but someone else always owned them. For most people, boats always require more money than the pleasure they produce.

Take Dave Ramsey's Financial Peace University course to help you in a step-by-step approach to getting out of debt and becoming financially free. Financial peace university: https://www.ramseysolutions.com/ramseyplus/financial-peace/

I created a plan to help my employees get out of debt as soon as possible. The greatest gift that I gave my employees is not being out of debt; the greatest gift is that I changed them from spenders to savers. This has done much to eliminate the money issues that many families argue about. The only drawback to this plan is that three out of the four team members who are now out of debt did not need to work as much and either now work part time in my practice or left the practice to enjoy their hobbies. Here is an example of one of those team members.

My chief clinical dental assistant was incredible at her job. She also had a hobby selling things on eBay. Surprisingly, she was making more than $50,000 a year in her hobby. Her husband was making about $15 an hour on his physically demanding construction job.

At age 32, they decided to live on his income and focus everything she earned from their eBay business and her salary from my dental office toward debt reduction and paying off their home. Using the system described in this book, they were able to pay off their mortgage in four years. My assistant then left my practice to focus her energies on building up their eBay company. They now work 20 hours a week living in their debt-free home and now have plenty of time for travel and enjoying the adventures of life as a family.

To ensure a comfortable retirement, they learned how to invest safely on their own, using the techniques described in this book. Over the next 30 years, they will accumulate a portfolio of more than $10 million, receiving more than $350,000 a year tax free from their solo Roth 401k plan.

Financial freedom is just a mindset and a numbers game. Once your plan is implemented, you will be debt free in 5 to 10 years. You can now stop worrying, focus on each day, and enjoy the process of life. **Appendix A: Step-By-Step Debt-Reduction Plan**

Appendix B: Ideas on How to Find and Make More Money (check out Rule One investing blog) https://www.ruleoneinvesting.com/blog/personal-development/ways-to-make-extra-money

CHAPTER 3

Learn How to Invest Safely and Simply on Your Own

A verse from the Eagles song "Already Gone" says "So often times it happens that we live our lives in chains, and we never even know we have the key." The key to your personal and financial independence is to get out of debt quickly and learn how to successfully invest on your own through undervalued wonderful companies.

While you are becoming debt free, you need to learn how to invest your money safely, on your own, without financial advisors and their outrageous management fees. This can be done risk free through paper trading, which will be described below. Learning how to invest in the stock market is like taking a college course in investing for a year. Is your financial freedom worth this amount of time? Here is a specific game plan to do this, reach your investment goals, and become financially free.

Disclaimer

I have found the following investment information to be helpful. I am not engaged in rendering professional services. If you require personal assistance or advice, seek a competent professional. I specifically disclaim any responsibility for any loss, liability, or risk, personal or otherwise, which is incurred directly or indirectly from the use and application of the contents of this book.

Rule One Investing

I'm about to share with you an easy-to-learn, effective investment strategy. This is much better than entrusting your funds to a financial advisor or fund manager who might end up taking 75% of the money you have earned. Yes, it requires some action, but what I'll guide you through is so straightforward that anyone, even those with no prior investment experience or aversion to math, can manage it. Using this approach, you could obtain an annual return of 15% which would be double the average market 7% return.

To make this happen for yourself, you need to understand the rules. Every successful investor, whether actively trading or a long-term investor, abides by Warren Buffet's two rules: rule #1—Don't lose money, and rule #2—Don't forget rule #1.

The embodiment of this philosophy can be found in the books written by Phil Town entitled: *Rule #1, Payback Time,* and *Invested*—all national bestsellers. In these books, he helps you find wonderful companies using technical tools to help you determine the true valuation of those companies so that you can purchase them at the best time at half price. This will be discussed in this chapter. Check out his website at: https://www.ruleoneinvesting.com/

If you want to retire financially independent, you must learn to grow your retirement funds on your own. This will also give you the extra funds needed to enjoy your life before you eventually step away from the workforce. Investing safely and predictably in the stock market is the fastest way to grow wealth through compound interest.

"Compound interest is the eighth wonder of the world. He who understands it, earns it . . . he who doesn't . . . pays it." —Albert Einstein. Here is a real-life example:

When I was at Command and General Staff College back in 1981, the post commander, LTG. Howard Stone, spoke to the entire school one afternoon on finances. He told us to pay attention to where we spend our money, and to put 10 to 15% toward debt reduction and savings. The savings money should now be put into an IRA. This will teach us the power of compound interest.

At that time, the maximum you could put in was $2,000, so I took $4,000 and funded my IRA for 1981 and 1982 with a broker at Edward Jones. He put me into a good loaded mutual fund that gave the same return as the S&P 500 index fund. That was the only time I ever invested in the market until the year 2000. General Stone wasn't around, so I never looked at or worried about that investment for 18 years.

In January 2000, I was shocked to see my $4,000 had grown $105,000, an overall return of twenty-six times. This is when I began to understand the power of compound interest. At a 15% annual return, that $105,000 would have grown from 2000 to 2022 to more than $3.2 million. Remember that this was a one-time investment of only $4,000, which grew to $3.2 million over 40 years. Just think how much I would have had if I had put in the maximum to my IRA account each year and understood how to invest it safely on my own.

Many individuals get confused with investing and do not understand how easy it is to invest on their own through a company like Charles Schwab. That is why they are so vulnerable to dangerous investment schemes and high-fee advisors and brokers that will destroy any chance for them to have a comfortable retirement.

> *The problem in America isn't so much what people*
> *don't know; the problem is what people*
> *think they know that just isn't so.*
> **—WILL ROGERS**

Everything you have been taught about money makes other people wealthy and keeps you poor. Learning to invest on your own and creating wealth is not complicated! The secret to becoming financially free is to make more money in your work and quickly pay off debt, receiving a guaranteed 100% tax-free return. During this time, you can learn how to trade in the stock market, using risk-free paper trading as described below. Also learn how to maximize your personal investments in a tax-free environment.

These options are never offered to you by your financial advisors because they can't make money from them. What you are offered are risky stocks and mutual funds with high commissions and advisory fees, along with the high anxiety associated with these products. The other supposedly safe type of investment is low-return bonds or treasuries, which will never provide adequate passive income for your life.

Most of your well-meaning advisors will not appreciate this paradigm shift, because each of them looks through a different lens based on their experience, training, and what they will make from you. Each has a different agenda for you and your money. You need to create your own agenda that works best for you.

Over the past 50 years, Americans have been taught by banks, the government, financial advisors, and financial institutions to stay in debt while telling them that the only way to become wealthy and retire comfortably is to accept risk, volatility, and unpredictability in the stock-market casino through 401(k) plans and other financial vehicles that they control.

If you follow their advice and investment models, they will take away two-thirds of your disposable income and freedom while keeping you broke, unable to retire and in debt for the rest of your life. You become their cash cow until you die.

You must first learn to focus all excess money on paying off all debt in 7 to 10 years. I will show you how to practice investing on your own, risk-free, through paper money, where you will learn the best strategies to safely get the best returns without any risk. You will no longer pay these extraordinarily high fees and commissions to financial advisors and brokers.

The Cost of Advisors

Below is a real example of an actively managed mutual fund *simple IRA* compared to the results of the S&P 500 fund over 12 years. In this true example, the individual would have had $706,742 rather than $342,445 (more than twice as much) if they would have just put their investments in the S&P 500 ETF (exchange traded fund).

The next real-life example is of a much larger office that maximized all tax-deductible strategies. On the left is the true account invested by their financial advisor in mutual funds. On the right is the result if they had invested on their own in the S&P 500 index fund, with an expense ratio of 0.03%. Just by investing on their own in the S&P 500, they would have had an annual 12.6% return with an ending balance in 2024 of more than $8.3 million in their 401(k) account. Compare this to their financial advisor's management of their portfolio resulting in an annual 7% return with a final balance of $4.25

YEAR	BROKERAGE ACCOUNT $ OPEN BAL	$ DEPOSITS	$ PRINCIPAL	RETURNS %	$	S&P 500 ACCOUNT $ OPEN BAL	$ DEPOSITS	$ PRINCIPAL	RETURNS % PRETAX	$ TREATED
2009	0	7,800	7,800	-0.81%	-63	0	7,800	7,800	26.46%	2,064
2010	7,737	14,950	22,687	5.98%	1,357	9,864	14,950	24,814	15.06%	3,737
2011	24,044	15,400	39,444	-2.44%	-963	28,551	15,400	43,951	2.11%	927
2012	38,481	14,950	53,431	9.99%	5,339	44,878	14,950	59,828	16.00%	9,573
2013	58,770	15,600	74,370	8.56%	6,368	69,401	15,600	85,001	32.39%	27,532
2014	80,738	15,750	96,488	2.86%	2,761	112,532	15,750	128,282	13.69%	17,562
2015	99,249	15,600	114,849	-4.34%	-4,984	145,844	15,600	161,444	1.38%	2,228
2016	109,865	16,900	126,765	6.95%	8,807	163,672	16,900	180,572	11.96%	21,596
2017	135,572	18,650	154,222	12.64%	19,499	202,169	18,650	220,819	21.83%	48,205
2018	173,721	15,654	189,375	-7.26%	-13,751	269,023	15,654	284,677	-4.38%	-12,469
2019	175,624	17,046	192,670	16.67%	32,112	272,209	17,046	289,255	31.49%	91,086
2020	224,782	19,520	244,302	11.24%	27,449	380,341	19,520	399,861	18.40%	73,574
2021	271,751	20,822	292,573	9.37%	27,427	473,435	20,822	494,257	28.71%	141,901
2022	320,000	21,076	341,076	-16.62%	-56,676	636,158	21,076	657,234	-18.11%	-119,025
2023	284,400	21,542	305,942	11.93%	36,503	538,209	21,542	559,751	26.26%	146,991
2024	342,445		342,445			706,742		706,742		

million. Over the past 12 years, they lost $4,051,981 (almost half) by allowing their financial advisors to manage their investments. The individual just now retired at age 65 and wishes he could go back 12 years and take control of his money back then. We need to learn how to invest safely on our own.

YEAR	BROKERAGE ACCOUNT $ OPEN BAL	$ DEPOSITS	$ PRINCIPAL	RETURNS %	$ GROWTH	S&P 500 ACCOUNT $ OPEN BAL	$ DEPOSITS	$ PRINCIPAL	RETURNS % PRETAX	$ GROWTH
2009	0	0	0		0	0	0		26.46%	#VALUE!
2010	0	0	0		768,319	0	0		15.06%	#VALUE!
2011	768,319	100,666	868,985	1.33%	11,596	768,319	100,666	868,985	2.11%	18,336
2012	880,581	105,482	986,063	7.97%	78,592	887,321	105,482	992,803	16.00%	158,848
2013	1,064,655	109,001	1,173,656	7.15%	83,897	1,151,651	109,001	1,260,652	32.39%	408,325
2014	1,257,553	120,592	1,378,145	6.80%	93,676	1,668,977	120,592	1,789,569	13.69%	244,992
2015	1,471,821	121,898	1,593,719	-5.96%	-94,920	2,034,561	121,898	2,156,459	1.38%	29,759
2016	1,498,799	424,999	1,923,798	1.25%	24,090	2,186,218	424,999	2,611,217	11.96%	312,302
2017	1,947,888	109,166	2,057,054	17.16%	352,940	2,923,519	109,166	3,032,685	21.83%	662,035
2018	2,409,994	102,891	2,512,885	-7.10%	-178,321	3,694,720	102,891	3,797,611	-4.38%	-166,335
2019	2,334,564	104,551	2,439,115	21.26%	518,571	3,631,276	104,551	3,735,827	31.49%	1,176,412
2020	2,957,686	87,991	3,045,677	21.91%	667,220	4,912,239	87,991	5,000,230	18.40%	920,042
2021	3,712,897	116,638	3,829,535	16.64%	637,293	5,920,272	116,638	6,036,910	28.71%	1,733,197
2022	4,466,828	115,769	4,582,597	-18.71%	-857,615	7,770,107	115,769	7,885,876	-18.11%	-1,428,132
2023	3,724,982	116,000	3,840,982	10.65%	409,018	6,457,743	116,000	6,573,743	26.29%	1,728,237
2024	4,250,000		4,250,000			8,301,981		8,301,981		

If you have a 401(k) plan, compare how your 401(k) plan has done compared to just investing in the S&P 500 index fund on your own. Do this now—don't wait until you're ready to retire. Go to: https://www.doctorace.com/resources/ and download the free Excel comparison sheet to see how your investments have done against the S&P 500 fund. Use your annual 5500, which is sent to the IRS each year to fill out this Excel sheet.

To obtain the 5500s, go to: https://www.efast.dol.gov/5500search/ and put in your EIN number to get copies of past 5500s. Go to Part III, 7a to find the beginning-of-the-year balance and next to that the end-of-the-year balance. The ending balance will be the same for the beginning balance of the next year. Then go to part 8a (1,2,3) to put in the total contributions that year. It is that simple. This will help you realize how much you have lost or gained in your retirement account by using the various advisors and mutual funds.

If you find that your advisors have done poorly compared to the S&P 500, you need to transfer your portfolio into an account that you have control of and on which you can make your own investment decisions. If this is not possible as an employee, then just put in the employer's match and place it into a low-cost index fund. If you are the employer, you may want to set up a self-directed 401(k) plan through Charles Schwab. Phone Schwab at 877-456-0777. https://www.youtube.com/watch?v=W7oVm3RJw_0

The late John Bogle, father of the indexed mutual fund, said in MarketWatch: "If you pay a hefty fee to an active manager, what happens to your potential return? Answer: Nothing good. A 2.5% fee over a typical investor's lifetime, an astounding 75% of compounding returns end up in the hands of the manager, not the investor." Bogle believes that actively managed funds are a big scam.

When you invest in loaded, actively managed mutual funds, you put up 100% of the capital and take 100% of the risk. If you make money, your fund manager takes up to 70% or more of the upside in fees. If you lose money, they still get paid. They are charging you 10 to 30 times what it would cost for you to buy a low-cost index fund that would match the market and beat 90% of the actively managed mutual funds.

Fees of only 1% per year can slash the value of your savings by 28% over the next 35 years, according to the Department of Labor. These are in addition to other fees in actively managed funds such as trading costs, taxes, and hidden fees.

Most individual investors put their money in mutual funds and rely upon money managers, financial advisors, and brokers who engage in hyperactive trading to try to beat the market by picking winners and timing. This is a losing strategy. More than 96% of investors would be better off consistently investing on their own in a S&P 500 index fund (SCHX or SWPPX).

Expenses and fees are the enemy of the individual investor. You must understand that advisors, brokers, and mutual-fund managers are well-meaning salespeople. If you invest on your own in an index S&P 500 fund at $4,000 per month for 30 years at 7% return, you will earn $3,781,475. What will your financial advisors, through their mutual fund, take from your earnings when they charge only 1%, 2%, 3% or 4% fees?

Advisory/Fund % fee	The money Advisory/Fund will take from you	% Return of your earnings
1%	$962,322	25%
2%	$1,725,989	46%
3%	$2,332,220	62%
4%	$2,820,600	75%

As you can see in the chart above, over time, these small percentages will take 25% to 75% of the profits from your investment, which kills the growth potential of your portfolio. Your advisors will always get paid, even when you lose money in market downturns.

> *"Unfortunately, the vast majority of those who bill themselves as financial advisors neither charge a fair price nor give good advice. More than any other market I know, the market for financial advice is 'Let the buyer beware.'"*
> —JIM DAHLE, MD

Remember, the person who cares the most about your money is you. Learn to invest on your own, and stay away from financial advisors and brokers who work on commission.

> *"You must unlearn what you have learned."*
> —YODA

As Yoda taught in *Star Wars*, the first step is letting go of how you have been programmed in the past. Take charge and control of your own money, and stop playing the bankers', advisors', and financial institutions' game. The new model described in this book will eliminate your money stress and bring peace back into your life.

How to Start Investing on Your Own

This chapter can be very confusing and scary for those who are unfamiliar with the stock market and the investing process.
The idea of investing on your own and understanding stocks and the stock market can be overwhelming. By learning to invest now, you will be able to create a constant source of increasing passive income for you and your family over your lifetime.

If you are not ready to take on this new adventure now, feel free to skim over this chapter and continue your reading at retirement plans and taxes on page 38.

Warren Buffett once said: "If you don't find a way to make money while you sleep, you will work until you die."

While you are spending your extra money paying off debt, learn how to invest on your own with a small amount of money or with paper money as described below. This chapter gives you an insight and overview of the investing process.

You do not have to be a genius to invest when you understand Rule One. It was created for the ordinary person just like you. Many people think you must take high risk to get high rewards in investing. This is just the opposite of Rule One investing. Here you can get high returns of 15% with low risk and reach retirement and financial independence a lot sooner.

Over the long run, investing in the stock market produces the best returns of any investment—better than bonds, better than gold, and even better than real estate if you do it the right way. When you buy stocks, you benefit in two ways: from any increases in the price of shares in the stock and from any dividends that the company pays to you as an investor.

To learn how to invest in the stock market and get the best returns, you will need a great teacher. I am not that teacher. But I can introduce you to my mentor, Phil Town, the founder of Rule One Investing. He will help and coach you through this process. He believes that, with the proper training, you could average more than 15% annual return on your investments in the stock market. I have found this to be true.

You will find much valuable information on his website, his books, and through his three-day virtual webinar. You are not going to learn how to best invest from this book or from any other book any more than you can learn to fly a plane by reading about flying in a book. You must go fly the plane and get the feel of it for real. To accelerate your learning experiences without making fateful mistakes, learn paper trading. This is taught in his hands-on Zoom course. Here you will learn a step-by-step approach on how to invest like Warren Buffett for only $97. These three days are your first step to financial freedom. https://www.ruleoneinvesting.com/virtual-investing-workshop/.

This Zoom course is the best I have ever taken to learn how to invest on my own without risk through paper trading. It is personally taught by Phil Town himself, along with his great instructors. In my small Zoom group of 8 students, we had two instructors to handhold us through each process and help you find great companies and buy them at half price.

Also check out his website and his blogs on learning to invest, financial control, stock basics, investment news and tips, retirement planning, and personal development. https://www.ruleoneinvesting.com/blog/stock-market-basics/become-investor/ https://www.ruleoneinvesting.com/blog/stock-market-basics/how-the-market-works/ https://www.ruleoneinvesting.com/blog/how-to-invest/value-investing/

You first need to set up an account in a brokerage house that has a great trading platform and the tools to help you understand when the best time is to get in or to get out of the market. I recommend Charles Schwab. I have no connection with Charles Schwab, other than I like and use their services. They have low or no fees for trading stocks, a user-friendly interface, easy-to-understand trading platform and incredible customer service.

It is an American multinational financial-services company. It offers banking, commercial banking, an electronic trading platform, and wealth-management advisory services to both retail and institutional clients. It has more than 360 branches, primarily in financial centers in the United States and the United Kingdom. It is the 13th largest banking institution in the United States, with more than $6.6 trillion in client assets. It is one of the three largest asset managers in the world.

Charles Schwab is open 24 hours a day, 7 days a week, and has excellent representatives and brokers. Schwab has no dollar minimums to open an account. It has one of the lowest expense ratios for the S&P 500 funds, and when you buy stocks and index ETFs (exchange-traded funds), there are no trading fees or commissions for any stocks or ETF trades.

While Schwab was designed to sell stocks and provide stock investors with the most current research and other useful information, they offer everything that any big bank would offer, including checking and savings accounts.

All representatives and Schwab brokers are salaried; they do not work on commission, so their advice focuses on your best interests. Schwab has agents located in most large cities. These local Schwab brokers can help you open an account, but it may be easier to go online and have an account set up within 30 minutes. You can call their online representative (800-435-4000) to help you through this process. Set up your Charles Schwab account: https://www.schwab.com/client-home

Once you set up an account, you'll then need to "fund" your Charles Schwab cash account (not margin account) by linking it to your personal bank accounts. Call up a Schwab representative to help you create this link. Within a day, you will be able to transfer money from your own bank account into your Schwab investment account. Once it is set up, then transfer the amount of money you plan to invest. You can also set up an automatic transfer each month if you would like. Initially there is no money needed to open an account.

Another option is to just send a check to Schwab. Check with a representative to verify the correct address to send the check, and write your name and account number on the check. After your brokerage account is set up, download the Charles Schwab app onto your phone.

They recently acquired Ameritrade and their trading platform, called *thinkorswim*. This is one of the best platforms to help you practice trading in the stock market without risk, using paper trades. Not only is it a great platform to determine when to buy in and get out of stocks but also for those who are interested in option trading. Ask your Schwab representative how to download and use *thinkorswim*. Check out the YouTube videos on how to use *thinkorswim*. This is your golden ticket to becoming a successful investor. https://www.youtube.com/watch?v=W5gJ5-p-8O8&list=PL5F91D714FC3CDE21&index=1

Understanding Rule One Investing

This system is not that hard to learn. My 12-year-old grandson is using what he learned in this course to invest in his Roth IRA. This is how you teach and create generational wealth. Of the many different investing strategies that a modern-day investor may choose, value investing is the best. It is also the foundation of the Rule One investing strategy. Once you learn this system, you will need to spend only 15 minutes a week possibly doing option trading and following the statistics of the 2 to 10 companies you own.

Here are the steps to Rule One investing. First, we must find a wonderful company. To help us, we use the Rule One toolbox to find the right company and create a watch list of these companies and the price you are willing to pay. These are the businesses you want to own and that you will buy if the price is right. Your Watch List won't be long. It may have one or two names on it. Over time, you may have only 5 to 10 companies that you own.

The toolbox will help us determine the true intrinsic retail value of the company. Next, we calculate the margin-of-safety price of these companies, and when the price drops to our margin-of-safety price, which is half of the retail value price, we buy the company. If the price continues to drop, then we buy more shares as long as it still remains a wonderful company. When the company grows to exceed 20% of the intrinsic retail value, we will sell the company. We use this money to buy other undervalued companies or to buy the same company when it is on sale for half price. We continue to do this until we are rich.

Our goal is to have 5 to 10 wonderful companies that we own. While we wait for the margin-of-safety price, we can do option trading. The Rule One course will teach you how to do option trading with very little risk, with a potential annual return of 20%. This takes only about 15 minutes per week to either see if the company is ready to buy or to put in your option trades.

Value investing is a strategy focusing on buying companies with a low price-to-earnings multiple. Ben Graham, Warren Buffett's mentor, is the father of value investing and wrote the bible of value investing, *Security Analysis*, in 1934. That book is still in print today.

He called this "value" investing because, ideally, each investment had more value than was paid in the price. In essence, the idea is to get $10 of value for a $5 price.

By the time Warren Buffett started investing money, though, the economy had changed, and finding deeply undervalued companies was not as easy as it had been in Graham's time. To adapt, Buffett adjusted the theory somewhat, choosing to focus on finding companies that were not only undervalued but were also wonderful businesses with a highly predictable future. Buffett also recommends that you buy only companies that you understand. He calls this your "circle of competence."

Rule One investing dictates that the best way to make large returns on your investments is to find a few intrinsically wonderful companies, run by good people and priced much lower than their actual value. A business that hits all these marks constitutes a Rule One company.

Qualities of a wonderful company. Their products are universal, they have honest management, can raise prices during inflationary times they maintain large profit margins and make the world a better place.

At its core, a Rule One stock is a company that is priced at half of its intrinsic value (fair market value/retail price). The problem is knowing what the true intrinsic value is. This term is thrown around a lot regarding value investing. The key is to buy companies at the margin-of-safety price, which is half of the intrinsic value price. One way of finding this is to use the Rule One toolbox.

Investors often make decisions like what Ben Graham did, based on the business looking cheap, but a Rule One investor knows that it is better to buy a wonderful business at a fair price than a fair business at a wonderful price.

This is why we as Rule One investors require a deep understanding of the companies we want to invest in. We must know the business well enough to know that it's wonderful. Understanding this mindset is an important step in learning value investing. While it may not appear all that complex, buying $10 bills for $5 can be an emotional challenge, but these mindset tips will help you master it.

Fear is your friend. Buffett said that the secret to great investing results is to buy when there is **Fear! Fear** is what makes the market price of a wonderful business fall substantially lower than its intrinsic value.

Focus on the Long Term. Buy businesses at the right time, and know that the right time will present itself if you're patient. Everyday stock market volatility and events such as recessions, market crashes, negative publicity, among others, create opportunities for value investors to jump in and buy when the price drops. We want to see the market go down so that we can pick up great companies at a significant discount.

Finding underpriced wonderful companies does not happen every day. Charlie Munger said we don't make money when we buy, and we don't make money when we sell; we make money when we wait. While we wait for the event, create a watch list of companies that we want to buy. During this time, we can use options to grow our money safely.

Use The 4-Ms

First you must ensure that the companies you are investing in are high-quality enough to retain their value throughout the time you are holding them. I like to evaluate whether a business is a wonderful company with what I call the 4-Ms of Investing: Meaning, Management, Moat, and Margin of Safety. Of the four, the margin of safety does not tell you if it is a good company, but it does help you buy these wonderful companies at half price.

Meaning—You must understand the meaning of the business. How does this industry work, who are the competitors, and how do they compete? And how does this business fit your personal values? Does it have meaning to you personally? This is important because if it has meaning to you, you'll better understand what it does and how it works. You'll be more likely to do the research necessary to understand all elements of the business that affect its value.

Management—The company needs to have management that is talented and has integrity. Perform a background check on the leaders in charge of guiding the company, paying close attention to their honesty, transparency, and success of their prior positions to determine if they are good, solid leaders that will take the company in the right direction. And, super critical, do they allocate capital well?

Moat—The company should have a moat. A moat is something intrinsic to business, making it very difficult for competitors to compete. If a company has patented technology, a network of users, control over the market, an impenetrable brand, or a product or service customers would never switch from, it has a moat. Commodity companies rarely have a moat and are not usually on our watch list.

Margin of Safety—To guarantee good returns, you must buy a company at a price that gives you a margin of safety. For Rule One investors, 50% off the value is the margin of safety to look for. This provides a buffer that makes it possible to still experience gains even if problems arise. This is the final M, but arguably the most important.

These 4-Ms separate Rule One investing from value investing. Both dictate that you must buy a company at a good price, but Rule One strategy requires a much deeper understanding of the business. We reduce risk with knowledge. That's the bottom line.

Research sources and websites—Today we have many great Internet resources to quickly look for and research wonderful companies. The best one I have found is the Rule One toolbox https://www.ruleonetoolbox.com/login . You can sign up for a 14-day free trial. The monthly cost is about $30.

Here you can get information that is hard to get anywhere else. It filters stocks based on specific parameters. You can search for the important numbers of great companies using the Rule One criteria for calculating growth rates, the moat and management numbers, and pricing and valuations. It even color codes the results so you can easily see which companies to look at or which companies you should avoid. You will learn how to use this toolbox when you take the Rule One virtual three-day course and receive a three-month subscription to the toolbox for free. https://www.youtube.com/watch?v=wmuPCLOo4U8&t=292s

The best resource for investment terminology is https://www.investopedia.com. Below are the best free investment research websites that I use and are very helpful. You can purchase upgrades for more in-depth research.

Charles Schwab (free)—https://client.schwab.com/app/research/#/tools/stocks
Seeking Alpha (free)—https://seekingalpha.com/
Yahoo finance (free)—https://finance.yahoo.com/

Red Flags—In chapter 5 of Phil Town's "Payback Time," he lists six red flags that you need to watch out for when selecting a company. The first is that it has no meaning to you. If you're not an expert in an industry, you don't have any business owning a company in that industry. Second, it has no moat. If there is no durable competitive advantage, don't even consider it. Without a moat, a business has to compete on price. Third, the CEO is a poor leader, without vision or strong values.

Fourth, the company cannot pay off its debt within three years. To check this, divide the total long-term debt by current earnings. Ideally, we would like to see no debt. Fifth, the company has powerful trade unions that can destroy their competitive edge. Sixth, be careful of technology companies, as their moat can disappear overnight with new technology.

Paper Trading

In the virtual course, you will learn how to set up a *thinkorswim* trading platform and use it to practice with paper money (you get $100,000 in Monopoly-like play money). This will help you overcome the fear of investing and the possibility of losing money while you learn how to invest safely. Once you open a trading account with Charles Schwab, call them and let them help you download the *thinkorswim* platform and show you how to make a paper trade. Set up your *thinkorswim* platform tools following the YouTube link below: https://www.youtube.com/watch?v=dr9r9AQL1p0

To paper-trade, you start by searching for a business that's wonderful and available at an attractive price. Use the toolbox to help you focus your search. Do the 4-M analysis on businesses until you find one that works for you. In your notebook, write down the name of the business and the symbol, the Sticker Price, and the MOS Price. Charles Schwab will usually start you out with $100,000 of fake money to practice with. Review the Tools for the businesses you want to buy, and when you have three Tools that say "Get in," buy the business on paper.

Open a Charles Schwab account for your children, and set up their own *thinkorswim* platform. Teach them to invest in the stock market without fear as well as the enjoyment and process of buying and selling stocks using paper money on *thinkorswim*. This will be better than any of the video games they're playing now.

Tools, FACs, and Trend Lines

Stocks move up or down, not so much to events that are happening. Events can and do affect the decision of the institutional fund manager to buy or sell the stocks, but, in the end, the price of the stock goes up or down only because of increased or decreased institutional investing. Because the big guys are more than 80% of the market, it takes them 6 to 12 weeks to get totally in or out of a company. For small investors like ourselves, it takes us only about 10 seconds to do the same.

Since January 2000 the S&P 500 has had an annualized rate of return, including reinvestment of dividends of 7.25%. Warren Buffett with Berkshire Hathaway had an annual return of around 10%. The problem with the S&P 500 is that it's over-diversified. And the reason Warren Buffett is unable to get the big returns as he did in the past is because he is too big and cannot move in and out of the market quickly like we can. We want to get a return of more than 15% a year or higher.

Being small gives us a great advantage over these large institutional investors. To help us identify when the big boys are getting in and out, we use tools known as technical indicators. There are three tools that are very helpful, and when all of them line up saying "buy," it's time to get in. When all three are saying "sell," it's time to get out. Simple.

Once you have identified a wonderful business that passes all 4-Ms and can buy it at 50% margin of safety, these tools help you have the courage to invest in those great companies. These tools are fantastic at keeping you from losing money if you are buying businesses at prices below their value (the sticker price). The only way to make money with certainty in any kind of investment is to buy it well below its value. Doing that will make you very rich.

The best source for these tools is at Charles Schwab through their trading platform called *thinkorswim*. Once you've downloaded the platform, use the following YouTube link to set up these tools correctly. https://www.youtube.com/watch?v=dr9r9AQL1p0. These tools are described in more detail in chapter 12 in Phil Town's book. *Rule #1: The Simple Strategy for Getting Rich—in Only 15 Minutes a Week!*

The first tool is called a moving average. This tool tracks the average price of a stock during a specific time period. Moving averages are simply closing prices over a defined number of days divided by that number of days. There are a lot of technical traders out there who trigger their buying and selling with a moving average. The moving average smooths out the peaks and valleys of daily price fluctuations and gives traders an easy view of the price trend.

Technical traders (which we are not) don't even think about what a business is worth. All they want to know is whether it's going to move up or down based on these or similar indicators. Technical traders make their buying and selling decisions based solely on price and do not undergo an analysis of the fundamentals of the company. They don't care about anything else except price movements. When the price line crosses above the moving average line, they buy. When the price line crosses below the moving average line, they sell.

The second tool is the MACD—Moving Average Convergence Divergence. Developed by an economist, Dr. Gerald Appel, the MACD is probably the most consistent indicator of significant trend changes in a stock, and it's certainly the most used technical indicator in the world. It looks at several price-average changes over time, generally in the short term. It shows us when momentum pressure is getting stronger either upward or downward. Since most of the money in the market is institutional, the MACD shows us when the big guys are sneaking in or sneaking out. The MACD is the combination of two moving averages—a fast one and a slow one—and how they interact.

The third tool is the slow stochastic, developed by Dr. George C. Lane. This is a momentum tool that tracks the overbuying and overselling of a stock. The Stochastic looks at the high price and the low price of a stock over a 14-trading-days period. When the price goes below the 20th percentile, the stock is getting oversold—too many sellers and not enough buyers.

When it moves up through the 20th percentile, it often means the big guys are starting to seriously buy and that the price is likely to go up as it came out of an oversold condition and moved toward more normal trading. When the price moves well above the 80th percentile, the stock is going into an overbought condition—too many buyers and not enough sellers. As it drops below the 80th percentile, it indicates the big guys were seriously taking profits and the price is likely to drop.

Here is an example of using *thinkorswim* and the three tools we have discussed set for monthly charting. Using T. Rowe Price as our example from

July 2019 until February 2024. In March 2019, you were able to see the three arrows going up and get in at $112. In December 2021, you saw the three arrows going down and you would have gotten out at $200. We then wait for the three arrows to go up in May 2023 and buy in at $108. In March 2019 the stochastic had no green arrow, but the line was moving upward, which qualifies as a green arrow.

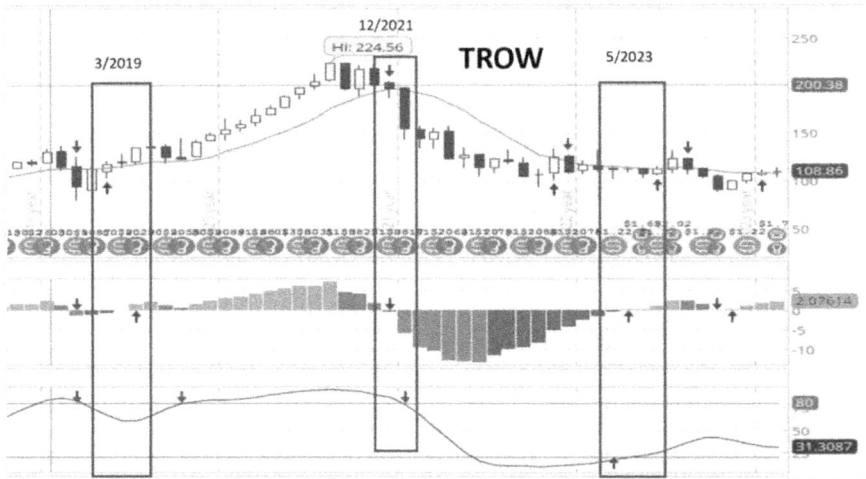

These tools can tell us when to buy and sell, but we need to first determine if this is a wonderful company to buy. Then we need to do our homework to determine the 4-Ms and the true intrinsic value of the company and buy it at half price. If we ignore the 4-Ms and accidentally buy businesses that are priced above their value, the prices of those businesses will eventually correct themselves downward toward the Sticker Price.

These tools are fantastic at keeping you from losing money if you are buying businesses at prices below their intrinsic value (the Sticker Price). The only way to make money with certainty in any kind of investment is to buy it well below its value. Doing that will make you very rich without taking the risk of being very poor.

The Floors and Ceilings (FACs) is a strategy for timing stock purchases based on the recurring patterns in a stock's price movement, utilizing psychological cues known as Floors and Ceilings (FACs). FACs play a crucial role in optimizing the timing of stockpiling, particularly when aiming for substantial discounts to the MOS (Margin of Safety) Price.

As value investors, we wait to buy a great company when it is at or below 50% of its sticker price, which is called margin of safety. At that time, we will stockpile. This is a term used to indicate initially putting a portion of our total capital we want to invest in the business, such as 25%. We then take advantage of the floors and ceilings lines to add another 25% or 50% as the stock drops lower and hits the floor.

FACs are rooted in the understanding that significant market players, such as fund managers controlling substantial sums in the market, tend to fixate on specific price targets. Although psychological in nature, FACs hold tangible significance. For instance, if a fund manager decides to buy a stock at $70 based on historical bounces at that price, it becomes a psychological floor in the price, akin to a solid foundation.

Observing any stock-price chart reveals that prices seldom ascend continuously; periodic reversals are inherent, even in bullish markets. These pullbacks are influenced by the emotions and psyche of investors, particularly the influential Big Guys. These market players may get apprehensive or overly optimistic, prompting them to initiate selling when they perceive a potential peak in the stock's price.

The time-consuming process of exiting positions requires anticipation of a mass exit, leading to selling actions. While selling safeguards against overstaying in the market, it also allows fund managers to realize profits. If the price stops declining after selling begins, fund managers might re-enter the market, starting another upward trajectory. The FACs stockpiling method labels a recurring price level a "Floor," signifying a point where a falling price tends to halt its descent.

A Floor is identified when the price consistently rebounds off a specific level without breaking downward. The frequency of these bounces determines the strength of the Floor. Conversely, when the price ceases its ascent and either descends or stabilizes, the FAC method designates this recurring level as a "Ceiling," implying a barrier that the price struggles to surpass.

Notably, when a price finally reaches a Ceiling and moves upward, the former Ceiling often transforms into a new Floor. Stock prices exhibit a somewhat consistent pattern of movement between Floors and Ceilings before breaking through or possibly retracing to test the previous Ceiling as a new Floor.

On a price chart depicting a business's stock-price evolution, Floors and Ceilings are visualized as horizontal lines representing points where the price halts and reverses direction, shaped by recurrent reversals at specific price levels.

An additional element to consider is the Trend lines, depicted diagonally on the chart; they serve as imaginary boundaries that form a Resistance at the top and a Support at the bottom. Trend lines are imaginary diagonal lines that form over a long time. Floor and Ceiling lines are imaginary horizontal lines that form over a short time.

While distinct from Floors and Ceilings, Trend lines are used similarly to predict potential price reversals, offering an additional layer of analysis for strategic decision-making. You can draw these floor and ceiling lines as well as trend lines using the drawing tools on your *thinkorswim* platform as you see below.

Fibonacci Retracements help us see Floors and Ceilings (FACs) that may not be obvious at first glance. You can create Fibonacci retracements in *thinkorswim* by drawing lines between the high and low time. Generally, use a six-to-nine-month time frame day chart, and try to look for the best fit. See example below.

To learn more, read chapter 6 in Phil Town's *Payback Time*. You will learn how to use these indicators during the three-day Rule One virtual workshop.

Three points to remember: 1. The more often the stock price bounces off the Floor or Ceiling, the stronger the Floor or Ceiling becomes. 2. To determine how far the price will climb from the new Floor to reach the next Ceiling, look at the distance between the last Floor and the last Ceiling. 3. A price move of more than 3 percent above the Ceiling or below the Floor, accompanied by 150 percent of the average daily volume of shares traded, is a significant sign of a breakout that will last.

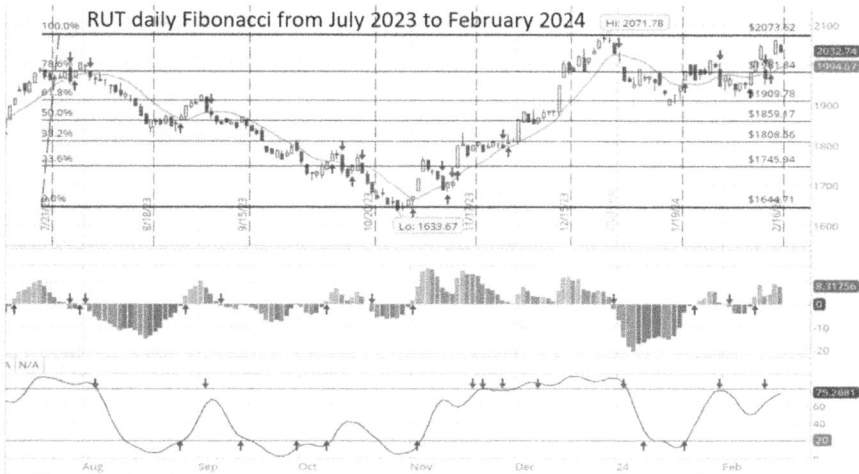

RUT daily Fibonacci from July 2023 to February 2024

The Floors and Ceilings (FACs) are predictable patterns in the price charts that show you the appropriate time to buy and sell. You can stockpile any time the price is below the MOS/Payback Time price but buying on the FACs will help you buy at the best possible price. To maximize your long-term investment returns. buy near the Floor price. Be patient!

Understanding Dividends

In today's investment landscape, there is a growing interest in acquiring stocks that offer dividends. It's appealing to possess ownership in a business and receive regular payments akin to holding a treasury bill. Some individuals even consider dividends as the primary incentive for owning shares in a public company, as it represents tangible cash returns from the business itself. Dividends are disbursed by public enterprises for two distinct reasons, with only one being a sound rationale.

I do not recommend the dividend reinvestment program (DRIP) because your dividends may be reinvested when the price of the stock is high. Use the cash dividends to live on, for option trading, or to purchase stocks that are undervalued.

The favorable reason is when a business accumulates more cash than it requires. A prudent CEO recognizes that this surplus belongs to the shareholders. The only justification for retaining it is if the CEO can utilize the funds to expand the business at a rate that justifies retaining the money. This growth rate is commonly known as Return on Equity (ROE), a critical metric. An effective CEO evaluates his team's performance, in part, based on how well they deploy owner capital. Indeed, overseeing the allocation of owner capital is arguably the CEO's most crucial responsibility. Returning the excess capital to shareholders becomes a legitimate option when the CEO cannot identify better investment opportunities.

The second reason is less commendable: some businesses allocate a portion of their earnings as a dividend to create the illusion of stability. This practice is influenced by Mr. Market, who prefers the appearance of steadiness over genuine stability. If earnings fluctuate, so does the dividend amount, causing unease for Mr. Market. He prefers a consistent dividend, resembling cash flow from a bond, and if this is achieved, he assigns a higher value to it. CEOs, responding to Mr. Market's preference, may establish an unwavering dividend quarter after quarter. This reliability attracts investors, especially retirees who mistakenly associate a consistent dividend with a stable business and therefore low risk. They don't want to sell the stock even if it's going down because they will miss out on their quarterly dividend payments.

Dividends make sense when a business has no superior alternatives for deploying your funds. For retirees relying on dividend income for their living expenses, investing in a robust business with consistent dividends is prudent, provided that these dividends stem from genuine, free cash flow. To ascertain whether dividends are derived from sources other than cash flow, a crucial step is to examine the Cash Flow Statement of the business.

Many retirees live on their dividends and unknowingly try to buy companies that pay a high dividend without realizing that they are losing money. When evaluating dividend-paying companies, the most important number to know is the annual equity yield, including reinvestment of dividend. The next important number is the dividend growth. The least important number is the dividend yield. Most investors focus on and want a high dividend yield. But as you can see from the chart below, the companies that had the lowest dividend yield gave the highest overall return.

Do not be fooled by high dividend yields, as many companies will increase their dividend yield each year to lull you into a false sense of security so you continue to hold the stock even as it continues to drop in value. Always evaluate the strength and growth of the company before you buy. Sell these companies when they start to drop in value and are no longer wonderful. Use the *thinkorswim* app to help you decide when the best time is to buy or sell. The annual growth of the company needs to be better than the S&P 500 as a guideline before you buy any dividend-paying companies. Check out the following sites.

To determine the stock's annual equity yield, including reinvestments of dividends, go to https://dqydj.com/stock-return-calculator/ To determine dividend growth and dividend yield, go to: https://seekingalpha.com/ .

The dividend yield is a stock's annual dividend payment as a percentage of the stock price per share. Most dividend investors look for a yield somewhere between 2.5% to 6%. But the best total overall return comes from companies that have a lower than 2.5% dividend yield.

You will notice in the chart below that the stock total return and dividend reinvestment came from those companies with lower dividend yields; they had the highest 10-year average dividend growth rates. Compare these companies with those on the bottom that have high dividend yield and low dividend growth rates. The average annual return, including dividend reinvestment on these high dividend yield companies (IBM, WBA, and LEG) over the past 10 years is only 1/10th the return of some of the lower-dividend-yield companies.

Broadcom ticker symbol AVGO dividend yield is 1.68% with a 10-year average dividend growth rate of 39% and an annual 10-year return of 39.5%. Over the past 10 years a onetime **initial $10,000 investment grew to more than $286,000** compared to Leggett & Platt, ticker symbol LEG, which had a 9.2% yield where the initial investment of $10,000 returned only $11,000 during that 10-year time frame, with dividends automatically reinvested. During the same time frame, the $10,000 placed in the S&P 500 grew 3 times to $33,000.

It is important to keep high-returning companies on your watch list and take advantage of them when they become undervalued. You must wait for an event, such as we saw in March 2020, when the S&P 500 dropped 37%. This was a great time to buy these companies. Another event occurred on March 2009. Many great companies such as Texas Instruments (TXN) and United Health (UNH) price dropped more than half in March 2009. Texas Instruments dropped to $14.00 a share but grew to more than $180 a share by 2022. United Health Group went from $16.00 a share in 2009 to $600 a share. Remember, "past performance is no guarantee of future results"!

You will also note that most of the selected dividend-growth companies in the chart have a higher average annual return than the S&P 500 or even Warren Buffett's Berkshire Hathaway company.

Dividend Example

Ticker Symbol	Company	Sector	Cur Price	Dividend Yield	Payout Ratio	10Y ADGR	Annual total % return 2014 to 2024	$10k Return 2014 to 2024	SA 10 yr Return	P/E <20	Rule one safety score
AVGO	Broadcom	IT	1250	1.68%	45%	39.0%	39.5%	286	2092%	24	88
MSFT	Microsoft	IT	406	0.74%	26%	10.2%	29.5%	132	970%	34	98
AMAT	Applied Materials	IT	185	0.71%	15%	12.0%	26.5%	104	844%	23	88
UNH	United Health	HC	515	1.45%	29%	21.4%	23.5%	82	600%	19	90
COST	Costco	CS	718	0.57%	27%	12.8%	23.0%	78	612%	45	80
HD	Home Depot	CD	357	2.34%	53%	18.2%	18.9%	56	360%	23	64
LOW	Lowe's	CD	226	1.95%	32%	18.9%	18.1%	52	355%	17	73
TXN	Texas Instruments	IT	157	2.82%	71%	22.4%	16.8%	47	267%	30	89
WSM	Williams Sonoma	CD	223	1.62%	23%	11.3%	16.3%	45	241%	15	97
BRK B	Berkshire Hathaway	ETF	396	0.00%	NA	NA	13.2%	34	250%	NA	NA
SPY	SPDR S&P 500 ETF	ETF	497	1.34%	NA	7.4%	12.6%	33	170%	NA	NA
IBM	IBM	IT	183	3.61%	69%	6.2%	4.5%	15	76%	18	27
LEG	Leggett & Platt	CD	19.7	9.20%	131%	4.4%	0.5%	11	111%	9	33
WBA	Walgreens Boots	CS	21.7	4.64%	55%	4.2%	-7.6%	5	-67%	7	30

Chart categories:

Cur Price: This is the current stock price (as of 14 February 2024). **Dividend Yield**: The current annual yield as a percentage (dividend/price x 100). **Payout Ratio**: This is the percentage of a company's earnings paid out in the form of a cash dividend. Ideally, we would like the payout to be less than 60%. **10Y AGDR** is the average annual dividend growth rate over the past 10 years. Dividend growth is the most important ingredient in successful dividend investing over time. Stock Total Return and Dividend Reinvestment (DRIP) average for 10 years from February 2014 to February 2024. https://dqydj.com/stock-return-calculator/

$10k Return 2014 to 2024: the total return in dollars with a $10,000 initial investment after 10 years. With AVGO, a $10,000 investment in 2014 would have grown to $286,000 in that 10 years. In 2014, a $10,000 investment with LEG would have grown to only $11,000 by 2024 in those 10 years.

SA 10 yr. Return: the total return on the stock after 10 years using the Seeking Alpha website. **PE<20**: This is the price-to-earnings ratio (price/earnings). Ideally we would like to see it below 20. **Rule One safety score**: this comes from the Rule One toolbox that rates all stocks. The highest obtainable rating of 100 indicates a very strong and safe company, such as Microsoft with a rating of 98, compared to a poor rating of 27 with IBM. The Rule One toolbox is a must for anyone who is involved in trading stocks. https://www. ruleonetoolbox.com/login

When to sell

Warren Buffett once remarked, "The best time to sell a wonderful business is never," this is because he owns part of or the entire company and retains control over its cash flow. As small investors, we can get in and out of the market in seconds, not like Warren Buffett who takes 6 to 12 weeks to sell or buy into a company.

There are three scenarios when we might want to sell our stocks.

The first one is when we need the money. Planning for the future is crucial, ensuring that when the day comes to sell, you have a range of options without significantly impacting your overall net worth. Anticipating this need allows you to select the businesses with the highest prices relative to their value, preventing forced sales during market downturns.

The second reason to sell is when the fundamentals of a once-wonderful company have changed, and it is no longer a wonderful company. Industries and businesses can evolve, losing their appeal due to technological advancements or other factors. Vigilance over the Big Five—industry and business fundamentals, Return on Invested Capital (ROIC), equity, cash flow, and debt—is essential. Any slippage in these areas, especially a decline in ROIC, serves as a red flag, indicating a potential need to exit. Use the Rule One toolbox to help you determine these numbers. Warren Buffett reminds us that if a business no longer aligns with your understanding or violates fundamental principles, it may be time to exit.

The third time we would sell is when the market price significantly exceeds the Sticker Price (retail value). While the initial approach involves buying at a low price, selling occurs when the price surpasses the Sticker Price (companies' intrinsic value price) by 20 percent. This strategy takes advantage of market euphoria, allowing you to potentially repurchase the business at a discount within a year or two, as Mr. Market's exuberance tends to be short-lived.

Why We Invest in the Stock Market

Over time, the best return on any investment has been in the stock market. At the beginning of the annual Berkshire Hathaway meeting in 2018, Warren Buffett wanted to share an important lesson with its shareholders. I will summarize what he said: *"Let's look back to 1942 when I bought my first stock and all the things that have happened since that time. We have had fourteen presidents, seven Republicans and seven Democrats. We had world wars, 9/11, Cuban missile crisis, and all kinds of terrible events that affected the market. But the best single thing you could have done on March 11, 1942 when I bought my first stock was to buy an index fund (Buffett specifically mentioned the S&P 500 index fund) and never, ever look at another headline. Just like you would have bought a farm and let the tenant farmer run it for you and never sell it. If you had put in $10,000 in an index fund at that time and reinvested the dividends, you would have $51 million today in 2018.*

If you took the same $10,000 and bought 300 ounces of gold, you would have only about $400,000 today. Gold does not produce anything, but businesses do. All you needed to do was to believe America would win the war and America would progress as it has ever since 1776. As America moves forward, American business moves forward. You didn't have to worry what stock to buy or what day to get in or out of the market or what the federal reserve would say. You just had to know that America works!"

The true compounded interest in the stock market over the last 120 years has only been 5%. As of the end of December 2023, the average yearly return of the S&P 500 is 10.54% over the last 100 years. This assumes dividends are reinvested. Dividends account for about 40% of the total gain over this period.

Adjusted for inflation, the 100-year average stock market return (including dividends) is 7.4%.

If that is the case, why not just buy the S&P 500 and never worry about learning how to invest on our own in the stock market? Why don't we just buy the Charles Schwab S&P 500 Index Fund (SWPPX), with a low expense ratio of .02%, or 2 basis points. This way, you don't have to understand or do any homework on the market.

The problem with this philosophy is that there are times when the S&P 500 does not go up at all for many years. These are called "long-term bear markets." The good news is that these bear markets are the best times for value investors to get great buys on wonderful companies through the Rule One investing philosophy.

Stock Cycles

Michael Alexander wrote a book entitled *Stock Cycles*. He reviews the markets over 200 years of American history until the year 2000. During that time, we have had seven long-term bear and seven long-term bull markets. The total average real return in a long-term bull market was 13.2%, while the average return in a long-term bear market was 0.3%.

For example, from 1929 to 1955 (25 years) it went up only 1.5%. From 1966 to 1982, the total real return was—1.5%. But from 1982 to the year 2000, the average total real return of the market was 14.8%. Alexander then went on to correctly predict that, starting in 2000, there would be a long-term bear market. In March 2013, the price of the Standard & Poor's (S&P) 500 was 1527, the same price as it was in March 2000, resulting in no growth of the stock, which is why those 12 years are called the lost decade.

From January 2011 up until January 2022 the S&P 500 average annual growth was about 14.5%, with reinvestment of dividends. The 18.11% drop with dividends reinvested of the S&P 500 in 2022 may have been an indication of a start of brand-new bear market. From January 2022 until January 2024, the return on the S&P 500 has been flat, at an annualized return (Dividends Reinvested) of 1.7%. No one can predict the market's direction, but the ups and downs of a bear market are the ideal landscape for Rule One investors.

There is a lot of talk about a new recession. One indication of recession has been the recent inversion of the yield curve, when long-term interest rates drop below short-term rates, indicating that investors are moving money away from short-term bonds and into long-term ones. This suggests that the market is becoming more pessimistic about the economic prospects for the near future.

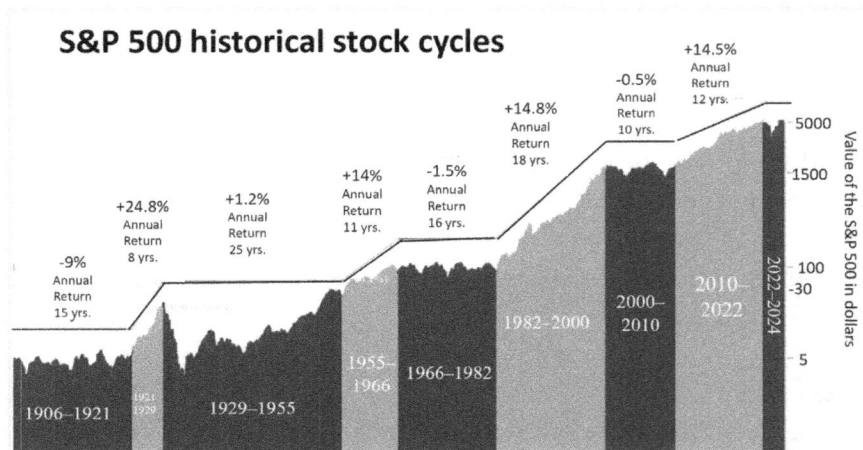

S&P 500 historical stock cycles

There are three other indicators that show the market is overvalued and that we may be in the beginning of a long, new-term bear market. These are the Buffett indicator, the Shiller P/E ratio, and the Wilshire GDP. As of January 31, 2024, the Buffett Indicator value was 184%, 1.6 standard deviations above the trend line, indicating the market is extremely overvalued. Dr. Shiller states that, when the P/E ratio of the S&P 500 is low (below 10), the market is undervalued. When the P/E ratio is above 20, the market is overvalued. In April 2024, the Shiller P/E ratio for the S&P 500 stands at 34, and the Wilshire GDP today is above 120% (extremely overvalued).

Long-term bear markets can be devastating for retirees, who no longer work and rely on their income from their stock portfolio. This type of market also affects anyone who passively puts their money in the S&P 500 or any mutual fund that matches the market index. But long-term bear markets are ideal for Rule One investors. During this time, there are many big ups and downs in the market, during which you can buy great companies significantly undervalued. In the last long bear market from 2000 to 2010, the market had two significant drops of 40% and 49%.

At the end of the long bear market in 2013, the price of the S&P 500 never got higher than the price it was in the year 2000. But during those

13 years, they were great opportunities for those who understood Rule One investing. In August 2007 Rule One investor Phil Town was interviewed on CNBC and recommended that we get out of the market. He used the three arrow indicators in *thinkorswim* to get out of the market in 2000 and 2007. These indicators also told him to get back in 2002 and make an 87% return and get out in 2007. Then he waited until 2009, when the three up-arrows told him to invest again and over the next three years had a return of 122%. See *thinkorswim* monthly graph below.

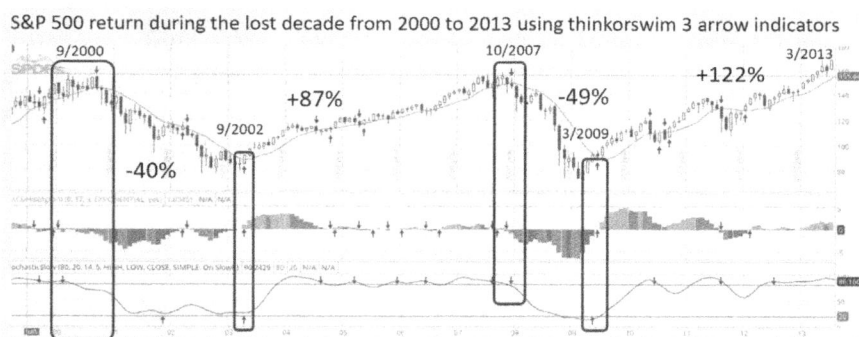

S&P 500 return during the lost decade from 2000 to 2013 using thinkorswim 3 arrow indicators

During this time, wonderful companies dropped to half their former size. Over the next 12 years, from 2011, their return on your investment was more than 10 times. This is why it is so important to learn how to invest safely on your own in the stock market and know when great companies go on sale.

For those of you who do not want to worry about researching companies and getting greater returns, then just buy the S&P 500 index fund (SWPPX). Use the *thinkorswim* trading platform, as seen above, to help you to get in and get out of the S&P 500 index fund at the best times.

Where to Put Your Money Now

As of April 2024, the market is at its all-time high, and we have yet to have an event where we can buy great companies at half price during the next long-term bear market. In order of preference, these are the following recommendations.

Finish paying off debt, which will give you the highest return while you learn to paper trade in the market through *thinkorswim*.

Schwab money market account (SWVXX) is a good interim place for your money while you are waiting to get into the market. As of this writing, their net return is about 5%. These are not FDIC insured, but they are SIPC insured up to $500,000. This fund is available for individual retirement and investment accounts. If your account is a corporation, a trust, or 401(k), then you would either use the Schwab Government Money Fund (SWVXX) or the Schwab Treasury Obligations Money Fund (SNOXX), also returning about 5%.

Option trading: The goal in Rule One investing is to buy 5 to 10 wonderful companies at the right price. This may take some time when the market is at its all-time high, like it is today. Option trades are done over a 5-day to a 30-day period, allowing your money to be available for those events where you can buy your wonderful company at half price. To make money while you wait, you may want to learn to do option trading. This is reviewed and discussed in the three-day virtual Zoom Rule One course.

Many option traders lose money because they have no system. In the course, you will learn specific rules to use for trading options that have been shown to have a 95% success rate, with a return of 15% to 30% a year. If done right, option trading can replace your income. As you practice paper trading, you will gain high confidence in the Rule One approach to option trading.

These trades are done with wonderful companies that you want to own anyway. They also have a two-year advanced course with excellent instructors for those who want to expand their investing knowledge and learn more about step-by-step option trading. Here you can practice with paper money in your simulated *thinkorswim* trading account with no risk. In 2023, the Rule One study group did more than 110 real option trades with only one loss (99% success) and annual return of more than 42%. It was a very good year.

Buy wonderful companies at half price. We must wait for an event to occur that pushes the stock to a half-price level. This can happen during volatile times, such as during a long bear market.

Enjoy the **passive income from dividends** you receive from those companies you already own.

Retirement Accounts and Taxes

To count on having a comfortable life and secure future in retirement, you must learn to invest on your own. This will ensure the maximum return on the money you have to invest. Passing on this responsibility to financial advisors to help you invest your savings will result in losing half or more of your retirement income.

There are 5 common mistakes you need to avoid while planning for retirement. The first mistake is not understanding how much you're going to need to retire. During retirement, you may have fewer expenses in some areas but other areas such as health care and travel will increase. Also, inflation will affect the buying power of your nest egg. Check out the investment calculator at: https://www.ruleoneinvesting.com/investment-calculators/

The second mistake is not taking advantage of your employer 401k matching money. Don't invest any more than is matched. The third mistake is relying on fund managers and advisors. You have the tools you need to learn to invest on your own on the internet. The next mistake is over-diversifying in many companies through index funds. Warren Buffett says diversification is for the ignorant. Focus on 4 to 6 individual wonderful companies that you understand and like. The final mistake is not researching these companies thoroughly and failure to understand the true intrinsic value so that you can purchase them at half price.

Investing in great companies is the best hedge against inflation and can be the best and safest place to put your money to beat inflation. Over the past 20 years, the inflation rate has been around 2.8%. In 2022, the inflation rate spiked to 9%, the highest inflation rate in 40 years, with no indication that it would fully subside soon.

If we could just buy and hold, there wouldn't be a tax issue. But sooner or later, we will want to spend the money. The big advantage of using the *thinkorswim* tools and three-arrow indicators is to help us get in and out of the market, with the big guys allowing us to make money while avoiding losing money. The only problem is when that money is in a taxable account, there can be long-term or short-term capital-gains taxes paid.

It is still better to make and keep your gains (profits) earned in the market and sell even if you must pay taxes. The strongest lesson we learn from Rule

One investing is that we can keep our excess money working for us through options doing one-week to one-month trades, but we will have to pay taxes. I would rather make 20 to 25% gains and pay taxes on it, versus making 0% and paying no taxes. Remember when your cash is in a money-market account, you will still be paying taxes on the interest earned.

The best choice is to be in a tax-free environment, that is why I encourage putting as much of your money in tax-free or deferred tax-free vehicles such as simple IRAs, Roth IRAs, SEP IRAs, 401ks, and backdoor Roth IRAs. Check out the different tax-deferred and tax-free options: https://www.ruleoneinvesting.com/blog/financial-control/investment-vehicles/. Here is another site: https://www.irs.gov/retirement-plans/cola-increases-for-dollar-limitations-on-benefits-and-contributions

Since I'm not a tax attorney or CPA, I'm not going to advise you about how to set up these plans. I will tell you I'm not a huge fan of most 401k plans that force you to invest in mutual funds. The only time a 401k is better than an IRA is when the company you work for matches at least 50 percent of the funds you put in there. In that case, take the free money, but put in only the amount they're going to match.

Tax Strategies to Help You Reduce or Eliminate All Taxes on Your Investments.

As an employer, you may want to start your own **self-directed safe harbor 401K** plan through Charles Schwab. This also has a Roth component. The employees will be given a range of different low-cost finds, including a money-market fund. Employers and other senior employees can have the option to self-direct their investments. Charles Schwab will introduce you to a plan administrator who will create the plan design and do the testing of the plan. The cost of setting up the plan and maintaining it ranges between $3000 and $6000 a year, depending on the number of employees. Call Schwab at 877 456-0777. If you are not happy with your high-fee, wealth-advisor-run plan, you can easily move it to a self-directed plan through Schwab. https://www.youtube.com/watch?v=W7oVm3RJw_0

Solo 401(k): If you are self-employed (one-person outfit, a freelancer, or an independent contractor) and don't employ others you can have a solo 401(k), also known as an independent 401(k) plan. Couples running businesses together also qualify. You can contribute to your solo 401(k) as both employer and employee. For 2024, you can contribute a combined total of $69,000. If you're age 50 or older, you can add another $7500. You can choose between a traditional plan or a Roth plan. I highly recommend that you make it a Roth 401(k). https://www.investopedia.com/ask/answers/100314/do-i-need-employer-set-401k-plan.asp

If you have money in a standard tax-deferred 401(k), you can convert all or part of the money into a Roth 401(k). When you do this, you will need to pay the tax on the money transferred at the end of the year when you receive your 1099. Would you rather pay the tax on $100,000 now or pay 50% tax on it as it grows to $3,000,000 in 20 years or $15,000,000 over the 30 years. This should not be a hard question to answer. Once your standard 401(k) is converted into a Roth 401(k), you will never pay any tax on the gains or withdrawal of the money.

Everyone should have a Roth IRA. If you make too much money for a Roth IRA, then open a standard IRA account, and fund the maximum allowable amount that year. Once funded into the account you can then transfer that money into a backdoor Roth IRA and pay the taxes.

Roth IRAs are tax-free forever! You put the money in after you pay tax on it, and it grows inside the Roth tax-free, and then, when you retire and take it out, you never have to pay tax on the gains. Teach your children how to invest using Rule One philosophy as you help them open and learn how to invest in their own Roth IRA account.

Any online brokerage can help you set up a Roth IRA over the phone. It's easy and takes a few minutes. They can also show you how to roll over a 401(k) that's no longer being matched by your employer. (Your accountant can help you determine which one is best for you, as well as how much you can allocate to it on an annual basis.)

Simple IRAs are also excellent—you can pack away a huge amount every year tax-free if you qualify. The key thing is to get the money into a tax-deferred or tax-free Roth account. Not all of the money we have to invest will be able to be put in a tax-free account. Some of the money you're investing might be in a taxable account. When you become debt free and have learned to invest through paper trading, you will create such an abundance, most of which will probably be in a taxable account. I don't mind being in the highest tax bracket because it means I'm making the most money.

Estate Planning and Asset Protection Checklist

Statistics show that, in 2023. about 25% of 18- to 54-year-olds have a will. 45% of people older than 55 have a will. 81% of people over the age of 72 have a will and only 18% were living trusts. It is also very important to have power of attorney for finance and healthcare directives. When you are debt free and have investments, you need to protect them and ensure they are passed down to your family with very little tax and no probate fees.

Without these items, there is a great possibility that, if something happens to you and your spouse, your drunken brother will take over all the money, spend it, and throw your kids out on the street. Think about it. Without a revocable living trust, your estate will go into probate, which makes all your assets public and is very expensive and emotionally draining to your heirs. It could take years before your estate is settled, thus depleting much of your estate's assets going to attorney fees.

I was working with a thirty-four-year-old dentist who was married and had a little girl, and one more child on the way. I told him to go to his local attorney and get these estate-planning documents drawn up. He said he would. Six months later, he was coming with his wife and team to one of my seminars in Seattle. During the flight, the plane had had a landing-gear issue, and they thought they would have to make a crash landing in Seattle. Fortunately, they got the gear down and landed safely. At the meeting, I asked him, "Don't you feel better now that you have your asset-protection plan in place?" He sheepishly said, "I will get those things done as soon as I get back."

Find a local attorney, and get these things done now:

- Durable power of attorney for healthcare

- Durable power of attorney for finances

- Living will

- Standard will

- Revocable living trust

For a less-expensive approach, you can also go to LegalZoom and set up one for as little as $250 with the help of their attorneys. https://www.legalzoom. com/personal/estate-planning

Make sure to update beneficiaries on all your banking and investment accounts. The beneficiaries get first claim, and those listed on the will are secondary.

Fill out a document locator that shows all of your assets, where important documents are located such as wills and trusts, your brokerage account and password, and all other important information needed by someone you trust such as your spouse, parents, or sibling in case something happens to you and/ or your spouse. This will be an important document for your family. You can download a free document locator at: https://doctorace.com/resources/

Just buy cheap term life insurance that will cover you until you're debt free and you have created a portfolio of investments that can give you and your family passive income for life.

Health Insurance is very important for financial security. An illness/ sickness can destroy you and your financial well-being for a decade or more. Try to remain under your parents' health insurance until you are at least 26 years old. Find a job that provides health insurance.

Should you buy or rent a home?

Bottom line: Do not purchase a home until your student loans are all paid off and you have at least a 20% down payment. The average American moves every seven years. By then, only 12% of the home is paid off with a 30-year mortgage. Then they get a new mortgage, starting all over again at 100%.

With a $280,000 mortgage over those seven years, they have only paid $34,257 toward their mortgage principal and lost $90,569 to the bank in interest. They also paid an additional 6% in sales commission ($16,800), $10,000 in home improvements, plus $4,000 in closing costs. **The bottom line: there was no increase in their net worth, and they will never, ever get out of debt.**

If they stay in the home and choose to pay back the original $280,000 loan at 4.9 % over the next 30 years, they will pay the $280,000 home price plus the $254,972 in interest, which equals $534,972 in after-tax money. I recommend that you never carry a mortgage larger than twice your gross income, and you should not spend more than 16% to 20% of your gross income on housing, including your mortgage payment, utilities, property tax, insurance, and maintenance.

Buy a home that is just large enough for your family and one that you can afford to pay off in 7 to 10 years. Make sure that you get a mortgage that has no penalty or fee for paying it off early. If you pay off the $280,000 home in seven years, you would only need to pay $51,225 in interest and would save an additional $203,647, which would've gone to interest. Now you can use this money to invest in your retirement plan. Check out: https://www.drcalculator.com/mortgage/old/

Remember: when buying a home over thirty years, most of the mortgage payments initially go to interest and very little goes to the principal (ownership) to pay off the home. For the first fifteen years, it's just like renting, except you have all the additional property taxes, maintenance, and homeowner's insurance. Beyond that, in most cases, you can't even write off the interest on your taxes because they are less than the standard deduction. You are much better off renting until you have a 20% down payment (to eliminate the need for private mortgage insurance) and can plan to pay off the house in 7 to 10 years.

Focus all excess money on those payments, and don't dilute your extra money by paying into children's college fund or into your retirement unless it's matched by your employer. Once you're debt-free and have maximized your retirement funding, then you can invest in your children's college funding.

When you buy a home, you now have real estate in your portfolio, and it becomes a form of forced savings, just like a long-term inflation-adjusted bond. And once it has been paid off, that money—which went to your mortgage payment—now can be used to invest in wonderful companies. Your paid-off home also becomes a safety net from which equity can be used in emergencies through home-equity loans.

The choice between buying a home and renting one is among the biggest financial decisions that many adults make. I would recommend renting if you do not plan to live in the house for longer than seven years.

Get rid of private mortgage insurance (PMI). If you did not have a 20% down payment when you purchased your house, you had to buy PMI, or private mortgage insurance. This is very expensive and a waste of money. It can cost you up to 1% of the loan amount annually. A $400,000 house will require $4,000 a year in insurance payments, or $333 in monthly payments. In accordance with the Homeowners Protection Act of 1998, your lender must terminate PMI on the date your loan balance is scheduled to reach 78% of the original value of your home (in other words, when your equity reaches 22%, provided you are current on your mortgage payments).

Call your lender, and ask them to cancel your PMI when you have paid down the mortgage balance to 80% of the home's original appraised value. You might have to write your lender a cancellation letter of the PMI. Accelerate your payments as fast as you can to eliminate the PMI and, once you've done this, you'll have an additional $333 a month to pay off your home early. https:/ www.investopedia.com/mortgage/ insurance/how-get-rid-pmi/

The Seven Principles of Investment and Debt

1. The key to financial freedom is to make more than you spend or spend less than you make.

2. Always save for consumption; never borrow for consumer items, vacations, and so forth. Pay off all credit cards and consumer debt in full each month.

3. Keep only the material possessions that add meaning to your life, and get rid of the rest—it is just junk.

4. Because your best source of money is your ability to earn it, focus on ways to increase your income: make yourself more valuable at your job, go back to school, or work part time until you become debt-free.

5. Only purchase a home that you can pay off in 7 to 10 years. Although it is not a liquid asset, it adds meaning to your life. When purchased properly, they can be good long-term investments and provide a hedge against inflation.

6. Learn how to invest on your own using the Rule One philosophy.

7. If you have it made, don't risk it. You now can save enough money to retire early if you just play it smart by paying off debt early and investing in wonderful companies at half price.

CHAPTER 4

Enjoy Life, Liberty, and the Pursuit of Happiness

Enjoying Good Health

About six years ago, I noticed that my computer IT guy had lost a considerable amount of weight. He was six foot two, and when I first met him, he weighed around 300 pounds. Within six months, he had dropped 100 pounds and now looked great. I was amazed because I disliked exercise and had always had trouble losing weight, so I asked him what his secret was.

He told me that weight loss was pretty much 90% diet and 10% exercise. He said he changed his eating habits and moved to a high-fat, low-carbohydrate, ketogenic method of eating. He recommended a site called Dietdoctor.com, which was founded in 2011 and has more than 55,000 members worldwide, making it the largest low-carb site in the world. It is filled with many articles, experts, videos, and low-carb recipes.

At that time, I was five foot six and weighed about 210 pounds, with a beautiful pot belly. Within three months of taking his advice, I lost more than 45 pounds and have maintained my weight at 165 pounds for the past six years. I walk a couple of miles once a week and do some weightlifting three times a week to keep my muscle tone. I take multivitamins, vitamin D, magnesium, and fish oil. I can now sleep eight hours a night, and I feel better than I have for years.

Another great website to help transform your health is http://drhyman.com/. Dr. Mark Hyman is an American physician and a *New York Times* best-selling author. He is the founder and medical director of the Ultra Wellness Center and director of the Cleveland Clinical Center for Functional Medicine.

Creating Great Relationships

Warren Buffett gives the following advice: *"Be around people that you admire and enjoy. They usually have an upbeat attitude about life, they're humorous, have integrity, and are generous people who are thinking about what they can do for you. These qualities that you admire are not innate at birth, and you can acquire them. Then there are those negative qualities that turn you off in people who always need to be right and whom you don't enjoy being with.*

You can choose what person you want to be, so why not choose the person you admire? Take your five best friends, mentors, or your heroes, and write down the qualities that you like about them. Incorporate these qualities in your life, and eliminate the qualities of the people who turn you off. It's that simple. It is important to work with people in your life, and you will get the best out of people if they like you. You need to develop these habits now. Incorporate the great qualities now, and eliminate the bad qualities, and you will have an incredible life. Choose your heroes very carefully because they will define you. You are one of your children's favorite heroes."

Buffett also said that the secret to long-lasting relationships is low expectations. A friend told me that relationships improved immensely when you give up the need to be right. Re-evaluate your community by listing the top five people you spend time with and ask, Do those relationships add to my future self?

Picking the right partner can be one of the most important financial decisions you'll ever make. Having too many successful marriages (divorces) can destroy your finances. Too many times, we get out of relationships for stupid reasons. Try to make it work. If you have wealth and are planning to get married, always have a good prenup agreement set up before the wedding date. If it is truly not working, and you are going to get a divorce, offer a fair and good settlement to your partner. If they are angry and only want to fight, tell your attorney to stop negotiating and get you in front of a judge. They will usually give you a fair settlement.

My wife, Nancy, and I were married in 1969. We have 5 children and 14 grandchildren. We have had our ups and downs, but we are very supportive of each other. And if she has a problem that I know I can fix immediately, I listen intently and never offer advice. (There is a great and funny YouTube clip by Jason Headly, called "It's Not About the Nail" that makes this point very clear.)

One last comment: I would never be in a relationship that is toxic or does not add true meaning to my life. Sadly, this toxicity could be from parents who are always judgmental and critical of you. Tell any toxic person that if they continue to be judgmental or critical, you will not be seeing them. I give you permission to take care of yourself first, or else you will not be good to anyone else. Think about what you are teaching your children about the type of relationship they should be in.

Learning and Understanding Meditation

Meditation helps reduce your stress, increase your energy, clear your brain and relax the body for a deeper, more restful sleep. It makes you feel more connected and less anxious, and helps you to be calmer and more clearheaded in demanding situations. It can help you experience better relationships and sharpen your life focus. To learn a simple and powerful form of meditation, I recommend the new book written by Emily Fletcher entitled, *Stress Less, Accomplish More: Meditation for Extraordinary Performance*. For a better understanding of the Ziva Technique of meditation, check out her website: https://zivameditation.com/online/ or watch her YouTube video https://www.youtube.com/watch?v=yy6uO0MzbPg.

Creating Love in Your Life

Love is that special feeling we get when we have a connection with people and things in our life. It is created when we initiate and give love to people and things. Somebody could love us, and yet we may not feel anything. But we always feel love when we are loving others. I am fortunate to be in a profession where we can love our patients, our team, what we do, and especially our family. This doesn't apply only to loving people but also to things in our lives such as a good movie, a book, a special mug, and other things we go back to and create that feeling of love. Like the movie, "Love, Actually," is all around us.

Letting Go of Issues and Emotional Pain from Your Past

When I was three years old, my mother divorced my father, and he moved to another city. My mother had to go back to school to get her degree, and my brothers and I lived with my grandmother for the next five years. At that young age, I subconsciously blamed myself for their divorce, because, if I could have been a better little boy, this would not have happened. I carried this shame and pain through adulthood, hoping that no one would find out how bad I was. I subconsciously stuffed this emotional pain and started to feel from my brain, not my heart, where there was no pain. This inability to feel deep emotions affected many in my personal and business relationships.

I can easily understand why many men are not emotional. Once I addressed the issue and let go of this emotional pain, which can be easily done with proper techniques, my life and I became more emotionally alive and peaceful. Many people carry deeply embedded emotional pain from their past that affects and controls their lives. This could be from abandonment (divorce), which I experienced, sexual abuse, not being wanted, and many more. One group I work with who are exceptionally good in helping individuals to identify, address, and let go of these issues is Legacy Life Consulting. Contact them at: https://www.legacylifeconsulting.com/ David Stamation (208) 946-3894.

You Need to Take Care of Yourself First

Many people feel they are serving others by giving away all their time and energies helping others, but by doing so, they are not taking care of themselves, leaving them feeling exhausted, frustrated, and angry. This is especially true with women. The sad part is, they could better serve and help others if they took care of their own needs first. They need to set time aside just for themselves to love and nurture themselves first—then they will feel much better, less resentful, and happier as they serve others. The magic phrase that they need to use more often is "No—I can't do that. Thanks for asking."

Teaching Your Children about Finances

Mahatma Gandhi was asked what his message to the world was. He said, "My life is my message." Teach your children the satisfaction of being a saver instead of a spender. You need to show them the satisfaction of accomplishment and doing a job well done. Be the example for them of how they can find fun and joy in everything they do, instead of teaching them duty, responsibility, and that you must work hard for a living.

Teach your children to understand the ideas in this book. Help your children find a job so that they learn to love work, save, and be disciplined with their money. Show them the power of getting out of debt and creating and funding their own Roth IRA. Teach them the value of money and the feeling of freedom associated with being debt free.

Stop Complaining

Half of the people think you deserve what you get, and the other half don't care. My mentor, Kendrick Mercer, shared a story with me after his three-month sailing from California to Lahaina, Maui. His trip was an incredible adventure, with beautiful sunny days, stormy weather, moonbows at night and wonderful solitude. After arriving in Lahaina, he took a plane to Honolulu. He was enjoying the view over the ocean while a lady sitting next to him was complaining to him about her life, children, and husband.

During the break in her conversation, he looked at her and said, "Let us play a game. Let us pretend the plane breaks right in half, and we are all going to die. All you see in front of you is blue sky. We have two choices: we can grab on to the armrest in terror and think about all the things we didn't do in our life, or we can calmly unbuckle our seatbelts, stand up, jump forward, and fly for the rest of our lives." She did not say much after that but gave him a big hug at the end of the flight. Why not live our life in gratitude and enjoy every moment?

How Do We Define Success?

This can be different for each one of us. For me, it is about loving what I do each day, being at peace in my life, being in good health, having time to be with and enjoy the people I love, being debt free, having enough money that I don't worry about money anymore, and having the time and resources to make a difference in the world around me.

Others may define success as being the best businessman, making a lot of money, having time to do missionary work, retiring at age fifty-five, having $2 million in the bank—the list goes on. This book is not meant to define your success but to show you how to have enough time and money to make choices in your life that are right for you. It is not about making a living. It is about making a life worth living.

French writer François-René de Chateaubriand (1768 to 1848) said, "A master in the art of living draws no sharp distinction between his work and his play; his labor and his leisure; his mind and his body; his education and his recreation. He hardly knows which is which; he simply pursues his vision of excellence through whatever he is doing and leaves others to determine whether he is working or playing. To himself, he always appears to be doing both."

How Much Is Enough?

If you are like most people in the world, one bowl of rice a day would be enough. Here in America, we think in terms of economic freedom. In my past book *Time and Money*, I define economic freedom as the day you have accumulated enough safe, liquid assets that can reproduce your lifestyle income (the amount of money it takes to maintain your lifestyle), with safeguards against inflation, for the rest of your life without touching the principal. This will vary by individual, but once you are debt free, you could reach that point in five to seven years, simply by following the recommendations in this book.

Make a Difference in the World

There is a difference between success and significance. One of the great advantages of having more time and more money is the ability to make a difference in the lives of people in the world around us. I believe that this brings even more abundance into our life. Even though you are working on paying off debt, donate either your time or money to an important cause. This will make a difference in your life and those you help.

The $2 Freedom and Happiness Bill

I love giving out $2 bills as a reminder of our freedom in the United States. This $2 bill is the only piece of US currency that depicts the same person on the front and standing on the back. On the front of the bill, we see Thomas Jefferson, the third president of the United States. Then we turn the bill over and him signing the Declaration of Independence. The people standing around the table are the committee who wrote the declaration. The main author is

Thomas Jefferson (the tall person in the center). The person standing on the far left is John Adams, the second president of the United States.

John Adams and Thomas Jefferson had a few things in common: They were both presidents and were the only presidents who signed the Declaration of Independence. They both died on July 4, 1826, within three hours of each other, exactly fifty years after they signed the Declaration of Independence.

In those days, the average man lived to age thirty-five. Adams was ninety, and Jefferson was eighty-three on the day they died. I believe the reason they lived two to three generations beyond the average man is that they were both highly motivated to instill and imprint the ideals of freedom and independence into our American culture. They lived with a purpose.

This is what makes the United States one of the freest countries in the world; we can work and live anywhere we want in this country. We are free to be in any mutual relationship that works, and we are free to leave ones that are toxic (a relationship where you will never grow and are always being put down).

Sadly, most Americans don't know they are free. Many feel trapped in their lives, business, jobs, and relationships. They feel angry, controlled, frustrated, anxious or sad. These feelings come from a place of fear—many people fear change and have one foot in and one foot out of their choices (relationships or jobs). These feelings immediately disappear when the person acts, after choosing to change, or by putting "both feet in or out" of their choice.

The $2 bill reminds us of our choice to be free, independent, and happy. The secret of happiness is in three choices. Any time you feel upset, angry, or trapped, there is something in your life that you are not accepting. The courage to make one of these three choices will give you back your freedom and peace of mind. The choices are as follows:

1. You can change your situation (relationship or work), which takes courage as you face and conquer your fears. For example, if someone is always judgmental or critical of you and this is a deal-breaker, then you can tell them that behavior is no longer acceptable to you and that, if they continue, you will leave the relationship. If they stop this unacceptable behavior, then you will stay and be at peace. If not, you choose number two.

2. You can leave the situation (i.e., relationship or work).

3. If you can't change the situation or you choose not to leave the situation, then you can stay and accept the "what is" of the situation and be totally at peace with the situation. Remember that you are the only one that is making you upset. This is an easy choice. You can totally be at peace in your life because it is just changing your mind. We need to change the wording from: "Why is this happening to me?" to "Why is this happening for me?"

Final Thoughts

Create a life you love. Make more money, and focus that money on debt reduction and your financial freedom. Once you are debt free, learn how to invest on your own in wonderful companies.

Stop listening to the news and worrying about what's happening in the market or the country. This is just noise. That's it. Now, enjoy your life, be grateful, and spend the rest of your money on things that add meaning to your life. This leads to financial freedom and a life of self-integrity and peace.

Economic peace of mind is more than just financial freedom. In fact, we can experience economic peace of mind long before we reach financial freedom. Once we have a solid guide in place for achieving financial freedom, we can let go of our anxiety about money and live as if it has already happened. With this newfound peace of mind, we can truly enjoy life in the moment because we are secure in what we have, and we know that we can deal with any life challenge.

Now we can face life with joy and excitement once we have a vision and a beautiful story for our lives. Remember that you have the canvas and you have the brush. Now create the most beautiful painting for your life.

Step-by-Step Debt-Reduction Plan

T o come up with an effective strategy for eliminating debt, it's important to have a clear sense of your monthly expenses and to determine how many of these expenses are payments on specific debts. Personal-finance software programs such as Mint.com or Microsoft Money can help you greatly in organizing this information on your computer.

First, write down all debts that you owe, along with the minimum payment for each debt, from the smallest to the largest (see below). We start with the smallest debt because we want to see results quickly, which helps us to continue the plan. Take 10% to 20% of what you make, and set up automatic payment through your bank, starting with the smallest debt. Once that's paid off, move on to the next debt. Continue this until all debt is paid off. You can write a check each month for the extra payment, but automatic payments are much more effective. Very important: All payments must be directed to the principal of the loan, not just to the loan. You will find an in-depth, step-by-step plan below.

Save unexpected extra money, tax returns, bonuses, and pay raises, and immediately use this "found money" to pay off your consumer debt. Look for areas in your expenses that you can reduce. Don't buy new cars. You can save thousands of dollars by buying a pre-owned car that is two to five years old. You may want to consider taking a second job for a short period of time to help eliminate credit-card debt. Some couples live on one salary and pay off debt with the other. Quality of life is found in our relationships, the experience, and the detail—not in the number of possessions we own. We need less to live on when we move from a materialistic life to one that is more inspirational and spiritual.

Act Today. Declaring that you are seriously committed to getting out of debt is the first step to achieving personal wealth. Go through the steps below. All forms can be downloaded from https://doctorace.com/resources/. Also check out the resource section for the debt-free millionaire program and the Smart wealth system.

1. **Sit down with your significant other:** Both of you must be on-board, knowing that this will strengthen your relationship, eliminate stress around money, and give you back your freedom. Then read this book together, and set time aside to do the following:

2. **Add up your net worth,** that is, everything you own, and then subtract everything you owe in the chart below.

Determine Your Net Worth			
Assets	**Amount**	**Liabilities**	**Amount**
Personal Cash (Bank)			
Business Cash (Bank)			
Taxable investments (stocks)			
Tax-deferred investments (IRA/401[k])			
Cash value life insurance			
Gold/Silver			
Other			
Real estate		How much is owed	
Main home		How much is owed	
Vacation homes		How much is owed	
Rental property		How much is owed	
Business building		How much is owed	
Business value		How much is owed	
Other Assets		How much is owed	
Automobiles/boat		How much is owed	
Personal property		How much is owed	
Pension (value = 20x yearly amt)		School loans	
Social Security (value = 20x yearly amount)		Credit card debt	
		Other debt	
Total assets $		Total liabilities $	
		Net worth $ (Assets Minus Liabilities)	

3. Write down your total household income.

Net income source (after taxes)	Earner A	Earner B
Salary (net, take-home pay)		
Part-time or self-employment income		
Home-based business income		
Investment income		
Social Security		
Pension		
Veteran's benefits		
Other		
Individual totals		
Total income of A and B		

4. **Reduce your monthly expenses.** List all your current monthly expenses in the "current" column below. In the "reduced" column, record the lowest amount you can reasonably spend on each item. Total up all "reduced" amounts at the bottom of column 3, and then subtract that amount from your total income. The resulting number is your maximum possible *found debt-reduction money*. Go through your credit-card receipts and checkbook, and add up all your monthly expenses. Use the list below. See where you can eliminate or reduce certain expenses. Those in **bold letters** are some of the best places to look for found money.

Monthly expenses	Current	Reduced
Retirement-plan contributions		
Going out for lunch at work		
Dining out (other than work lunches)		
Groceries (use coupons)		
Telephone (including cell phone)		
Heating fuel		
Water/sewer		
Electricity		
Car cost (fuel and maintenance)		
Parking, tolls, etc. (carpool or bus)		
Car #1 payment		
Car #2 payment		
Insurance—automobile (higher deductibles)		
Insurance—health (higher deductibles)		
Insurance—home (umbrella insurance)		
Insurance—other		
Home-equity loan payment		
Re-finance home mortgage (walk away)		
Other loan payment		
Child care		
Cable or satellite TV		

Monthly expenses	Current	Reduced
Movies		
DVD rental		
Other entertainment		
Sports (golf, fishing, etc.)		
Health club		
Lawn maintenance		
Laundry and dry cleaning		
Pet food and care		
Subscriptions		
Online computer services		
Credit-card payment		
Credit-card payment		
Credit-card payment		
Christmas gifts		
College education for children		
Private schools		
Emergency fund		
Other savings		
Total reduced monthly expenses =		

Total income minus reduced monthly expenses = _____
(this is your *found debt-reduction money* used to accelerate your
debt payments)

> 5. **Develop a spending journal,** and for a month, write down
> each purchase you make (except regularly scheduled bills). This

includes incidentals such as coffee, parking, and other items less than a dollar. Use mint.com or download from https:// doctorace.com/resources/

Date	Item purchased	Cash	Credit	Check	Amount

6. **Your Debt-elimination Worksheet** (described below) to pay off all debts within seven to ten years. Read through the debt-elimination-approach description, and then fill out the debt form to see how long it will take you to pay off all debts by making a 10% or 20% payment toward debt each month. I am not a big fan of budgeting. If you are serious about getting out of debt, automatically take 10% or 20% out of your bank account each month, as if it were a tax. Live on the rest. **Automation of the payments is the secret!** Filling out the form below will help you understand your financial goals.

Debt Elimination Worksheet

dentify your debts, and record them on the Debt-elimination Worksheet below (you can go to https://doctorace.com/resources/ and download the worksheet). First, pay all small debts (less than $10,000) starting with the smallest. This "small debt" category includes credit-card debt, consumer debt, auto-loan balances and small student loans. Start with the smallest debt (no matter how high or low the interest), and then use the money from your *debt-reduction savings account* to pay it off first, while continuing to make the minimum payments on your other debts.

At the beginning, it's important to get momentum and see that you are making progress, so don't worry about the respective interest rates now. If the high credit-card-interest rate on a larger debt bothers you, you can always call the company and successfully negotiate a lower rate or transfer your balance to another credit-card company with a lower rate.

Once you have paid off the first debt, you'll feel a sense of empowerment. Paying off that debt frees up additional money, which you add to your savings. Use this increased savings to pay down the next-smallest debt. Fill out the worksheet in pencil so that you can update it each month. This will help you keep on track and stay motivated.

As you pay down debt, you gain momentum and free up more money to pay off the next debt. The money that pays off these debts comes from increased income, reduced spending, and the extra money that becomes available as you pay off each debt. If you have money saved when you begin setting in motion *Dr. Ace's Financial Freedom Guide*, for the sake of your peace of mind, do *not* use that money for early debt reduction for at least six months. Below is an example of how we pay off debt.

First, determine what percentage of income you want to pay toward debt. If you and your spouse's average income is $72,000, you would divide this by 12 months, giving you $6,000; after taxes, that would be $5,000. 10% of this would be $500 per month.

The $500 (10%) will be paid each month to the principal of the top loan in the chart. First, add the $500 to the Visa card $30 payment, giving you $530 per month to pay toward that loan, which will be paid off in two months. When the Visa card is paid off, apply that $530 plus $32 to the next MasterCard loan, which will result in $562; it will take three months to pay off *that* loan. Your efforts will continue to eliminate all your debt. The debts will be paid off in seven years and four months, and you will have an extra $31,176 per year to invest, save, take vacations, send children through college, or work less.

$500 (10%) Paid Monthly to the Principal of Top Loan in the Chart

Name of Debt	Total Balance (smallest to largest)	Monthly Payment	Accelerated Monthly Payment	Months to pay off
VISA Card	$1,000	$30	$530	2
MasterCard	$1,500	$32	$562	3
Department store	$2,000	$36	$598	4
Car 1	$9,200	$520	$1,118	9
Car 2	$14,300	$750	$1,868	8
Home-equity loan	$26,000	$370	$2,238	12
Mortgage at 4.5%	$155,000	$860	$3,098	50
Totals	$209,000	$2,598 ($31,176/yr.)		88 months (7 yrs. 4 mo.)

$1,000 (20%) Paid Monthly to the Principal of Top Loan in the Chart

Name of Debt	Total Balance (smallest to largest)	Monthly Payment	Accelerated Monthly Payment	Months to pay off
VISA Card	$1,000	$30	$1,030	1
MasterCard	$1,500	$32	$1,062	2
Department store	$2,000	$36	$1,098	2
Car 1	$9,200	$520	$1,618	6
Car 2	$14,300	$750	$2,368	6
Home-equity loan	$26,000	$370	$2,738	10
Mortgage at 4.5%	$155,000	$860	$3,098	43
Totals	$209,000	$2,598 ($31,176/yr.)		70 months (5 yrs. 7 mo.)

Your Debt-Elimination Worksheet: Calculate Paying Off Your Debt
(Annual household income: $ _____)
(Average American debt is 2.5 times the annual household income)

1. **Determine your extra monthly payments: $_____**
   Try for 10% or more of your monthly take-home income. If you have only a home mortgage, then you should add 20% to 30% of your monthly take-home income.

2. **Write down each debt in the first column below,** prioritizing each debt from smallest to largest. Do not be concerned about the interest rate.

3. **Using the debt-elimination approach, add your accelerator margin to the smallest debt,** making this new monthly payment. Put this in column 4. To determine when the debt will be paid off, divide this amount into the total balance of that debt by the new monthly payment in column 4, and put the number of months to pay off in column 5.

4. **When this debt is paid off, add what used to be the monthly payment amount to the next-smallest debt** payment, and

place that in column 4. Again, divide this amount into the total balance of that debt by your new monthly payment in column 4. Put the number of months to pay off in column 5.

5.   **Continue adding each paid-off debt's monthly payment amount to its accelerated monthly payment** and rolling the total amount to the next debt.

6.   **Add up the months in column 5 to determine when all debts will be paid off.**

Name of Debt	Total Balance	Monthly Payment	Accelerated Monthly Payment	Months to Pay Off
1	2	3	4	5
Totals				

Things to keep in mind about your debt-elimination plan:

- Use only minimum payments to maximize the debt-elimination process.

- Use only the principal and interest portion of your mortgage payment (not tax/insurance).

- Interest rates are not a big factor.

- Only non-recurring debts go into your debt-elimination plan.

7. **Write and post your Financial Goals.** I am taking 10% of my income and paying off my debts. In six months (date), I will use 20% of my income toward an extra payment on my debts. I will pay off all credit-card debt in one year (date), my car in two years (date) and my home in six years (date). Each month, review and challenge yourself to increase your debt reduction.

8. **Develop a support group of either family or coworkers**. Most families' money issues cause the greatest stress, and most do not understand how debt can keep a person in prison and take two thirds of their income throughout their lifetime. In my office, I created and presented to my team and their spouse a debt-reduction plan, which you will find at https://doctorace. com/resources/. In this program I showed them how to pay off debt, including their home, within 10 years, thereby freeing up more money to invest in their retirement fund. I also showed them how to invest safely with little risk and higher returns. Within six years, I have four of my employees completely out of debt, including their home, and the others have a game plan to be debt free within the next 10 years.

9. **Continue to read books** and listen to audios and watch the videos on debt reduction, including the ones found at https:// doctorace.com/resources/

10. **Take Dave Ramsey's Financial Peace University** course to help you in a step-by-step approach to getting out of debt and becoming financially free. Financial peace university. https://www.ramseysolutions.com/ramseyplus/financial-peace/

11. **Become the teacher.** First set up and start the program yourself. Bring your family and friends together and watch these videos. Pass out the handouts and help them set up the program for themselves. Share other debt-reduction resources with them. Share this material within your community, and help them regain their freedom.

12. **Celebrate Success.** This is *not* a no-spending plan; it is a managed-spending plan. I am not saying you can't spend any money on the things you want . . . But I *do* want you to be aware of the impact that each expenditure has on your ability to build your wealth. Most people can easily spend and live on half the amount they normally spend.

Managing Bumps in the Road

I f you have an emergency during this time—for example, major car repairs or unexpected medical bills—you can use your paid-off credit card or skip a month or two of debt-reduction payments and use the cash that would have gone toward debts to cover the emergency. The same is true if you feel you need an inexpensive vacation: skip a month or two of debt reduction, and pay for your vacation with cash. Just be sure to get back on track with your debt-reduction plan as soon as you can. I do *not* believe that you must have an emergency fund for you to start debt reduction. Some consultants recommend three to six months of income, but if you wait for that, it might take you two or three years to start your debt-reduction program. Once you have a paid-off credit card, you *do* have an emergency fund.

Once you've made progress paying down your small debt, be sure to fund your Roth IRA and any pension plan at work up to the limit that the company matches your money. Try to fund all company-matched IRA in a Roth IRA.

As soon as you've paid off all your small debts (less than $10,000), celebrate! Now take the "found money" you have freed up, and use it to pay off large debts (more than $10,000), such as your car loan, your home mortgage, and any lines of credit. This may seem like a slow process, but once you've paid off all your debts and are regularly investing in your retirement funds, you'll have a considerable amount of excess money left each month to invest in the investment strategies described later in this book. By following this plan, most people can pay off all their credit-card debt in one year and their car in the second year. By the third year, they are making extra payments toward the principal on their mortgage. Most people following this plan can be debt free and pay off their home in seven to ten years.

When your last debt (home) is paid off, 40% to 60% of your income will be available for investments or to place into your savings. This will allow you to become totally financially free in another eight or nine years. Figures 3 and 4 are examples of the debt-elimination approach to paying off your debts.

Ideas on How to Find and Make More Money

✓ https://www.ruleoneinvesting.com/blog/personal-development /ways-to-make-extra-money/

✓ An extra job becomes the rocket booster to accelerate your debt reduction.

✓ Make more at your job and put it toward debt.

✓ Do consulting work from home.

✓ Set up an eBay account and business.

✓ Learn how to create an online business at home.

✓ Go to clients at their home (bookkeepers or computer experts).

✓ Teach college at night.

✓ Check out internet on "work-at-home jobs" (beware of scams).

✓ Multilevel marketing (e.g., Mary Kay) (beware of scams).

✓ Go back to school to give you opportunities for a higher-paying job, and make all efforts to limit your student loan debts.

✓ With an extra job, you could be debt free three years earlier.

Other ideas for finding extra money.

✓ Stop funding retirement until debt free, except for matching contributions.

✓ Get rid of your emergency fund. Once your credit card is paid, it becomes your emergency fund.

✓ Evaluate/reduce holiday gift giving.

✓ Check bank/credit-card statement.

✓ Stop smoking.

✓ Properly maintain your home and car.

✓ Never buy a brand-new car until debt free.

✓ Never finance beyond 36 months.

✓ Take advantage of "cheap," meaningful vacations.

✓ Don't buy tools/boats you don't often use—rent or borrow them.

✓ Conserve utility usage.

✓ Avoid "Retail Therapy."

✓ Learn to say "No" to kids.

✓ Think like Warren Buffett, and send your children to public grade schools and high schools instead of private schools.

✓ Stop funding your children's education. Let them pay for college and apply for as many scholarships as they can. Many scholarships never get applied for.

✓ Apply all bonuses and pay raises toward debt.

✓ Eliminate private mortgage insurance (PMI) by paying down the mortgage balance to 80% of the home's original appraised value.

✓ Evaluate your real insurance needs.

✓ Auto insurance: get higher deductibles.

✓ Personal-liability insurance.

✓ Medical insurance.

✓ Get higher deductibles.

✓ Get an umbrella attachment.

✓ Never buy extended warranties.

✓ Use coupons (retailmenot.com, Joinhoney.com).

✓ Stop getting tax refunds.

✓ Spare-change jar.

✓ Have only a cell phone.

✓ Minimize dining out. Move to brown-bag lunches.

✓ Simplified lifestyle.

✓ Entertainment—Movies—Get rid of cable.

✓ Shop at outlet malls/Goodwill.

✓ See if you can refinance your home at a lower rate without fees through Quicken loans or a local bank.

✓ Buy a duplex and live on one side; use your renter payment to double your monthly mortgage payments. Look at prebuilt homes as a starter home.

✓ One of the fastest ways to become debt free is to move to a cheaper location. The average home price in the U.S. is $348,500 in 2024. It is a lot easier to get out of debt if you buy your home in a location where the home prices are low, such as in West Virginia for $143,200, Indiana and Ohio at $180,000 compared to San Jose, California, where the average home is $1,406,957.

This is *not* a no-spending plan; it is a managed-spending plan. I am not saying you can't spend any money on the things you want. But I *do* want you to be aware of the impact that each expenditure has on your ability to build your wealth. Most people can easily spend and live on half the amount they normally spend.

www.ingramcontent.com/pod-product-compliance
Lightning Source LLC
Chambersburg PA
CBHW031907200326
41597CB00012B/546